The Spirit of Ozark Distillery

A Culinary Adventure

David W Huffman Sr

Printed Worldwide
First Printing 2023
First Edition 2023

10 9 8 7 6 5 4 3 2 1

The Spirit of Ozark Distillery

TABLE OF CONTENTS

INTRODUCTION

Ozark Distillery is a small, craft distillery known for its handcrafted spirits located in the Lake of the Ozarks area of Missouri. It is a family-owned business that prides itself on using traditional distillation methods to produce a variety of spirits including bourbon whiskey, vodka, and a selection of moonshines.

One of the standout features of Ozark Distillery is their use of local ingredients, which allows them to capture the essence of the Ozarks in every bottle. This commitment to local sourcing is not just about quality; it's also about supporting the community and the local economy.

The distillery offers a range of flavored moonshines, a nod to the rich moonshining traditions in the Ozark region. These moonshines feature unique and regional flavors, including classics like apple pie and more creative ventures such as salted caramel, reflecting the innovative spirit of the distillery.

Ozark Distillery also offers tours on Saturday's providing visitors with an immersive experience where they can learn about the distillation process, the history of the craft in the region, and the story behind the distillery itself. During these visits, guests can sample the distillery's offerings and gain insight into the subtle nuances that make each spirit unique.

The distillery's products have gained a loyal following for their quality and the company's commitment to the craft, with a particular emphasis on the character and tradition of Ozark's spirit-making heritage.

"The Spirit of Ozark Distillery: A Culinary Adventure" is not just a cookbook, but a journey—a voyage through flavors, traditions, and the intoxicating allure of the beverages that have made Ozark Distillery a household name.

In these pages, you'll find more than just recipes, we like to throw in a little fun; from the warming embrace of our signature bourbon whiskey to the invigorating kick of our Spicy Bloody Mary Mix, Ozark Distillery spirits seamlessly infuse every dish with a unique touch, turning ordinary recipes into extraordinary experiences. But, there's no pictures! We don't take very good pictures and didn't want to use the fake pictures most recipe books use and besides, you all know what food looks like!

Whether you're a seasoned chef, a cocktail enthusiast, or someone simply looking to explore new culinary horizons, this cookbook offers a down home guide to infusing your dishes with the authentic taste of the Ozarks. Delight in main courses, desserts, and our distillery cocktail menu all elevated by the distinct flavors of Ozark Distillery. Celebrate the convergence of tradition and innovation, and let's embark on this flavorful journey together. Experience Ozark Distillery like never before, one plate at time!

OZARK DISTILLERY

"We don't compete, we create."

- David W Huffman Sr

The following is our Ozark Distillery Drink Menu including all the signature drinks we serve at the distillery. We set out to create simple cocktails with one or two ingredients. Enjoy!

OZARK DISTILLERY APPLE PIE MOONSHINE

APPLE PIE ALA MODE

Indulge in the warm, comforting flavors of apple pie with a delicious twist. This Moonshine Apple Pie recipe combines the sweet notes of Ozark Distillery's Apple Pie Moonshine with cream soda. It's a perfect drink for a cozy evening with friends or a special dessert-themed gathering.

1 ½ oz Ozark Distillery Apple Pie Moonshine

5 oz Cream Soda

Apple slice

Fill rocks glass with ice, add Apple Pie Moonshine and cream soda. Garnish with an apple slice.

CRANAPPLE SPRITZER

CranApple Spritzer enhanced with the warm, spicy fragrance of Ozark Distillery's Apple Pie Moonshine, is a delectable explosion of fall flavors. This cocktail creates a crisp, refreshing, and cozy beverage that goes well with any meal by combining the tartness of cranberry juice with the sweet fizz of Sprite.

1 ½ oz Ozark Distillery Apple Pie Moonshine

5 oz Cranberry Juice

Sprite

Fill rocks glass with ice. Add Apple Pie Moonshine, cranberry juice and a splash of sprite. Garnish with an apple slice.

OZARK DISTILLERY BLACKBERRY MOONSHINE

WOOBLY BOOT

The Woobly Boot Blackberry Moonshine Cocktail blends the fruity undertones of Ozark Distillery's Blackberry Moonshine with the taste of lemonade for a cool, refreshing drink. For a sunny afternoon, a backyard BBQ, or any other occasion where you want a little Southern charm in your glass, this delectable and simple-to-make beverage is ideal. A Summertime favorite!

1 ½ oz Ozark Distillery Blackberry Moonshine

5 oz Lemonade

Fill a glass with ice. Add Blackberry Moonshine, lemonade and garnish with a lemon wheel.

BLACKBERRY MARGARITA

Ozark Distillery's Blackberry Margarita is a delicious take on the classic margarita that is infused with its rich fruity blackberry notes. To enjoy a combination of sweet and spicy flavors and is sure to become a new favorite. It is will add excitement to your day whether you are celebrating a special occasion or just relaxing!

1 ¾ oz Ozark Distillery Blackberry Moonshine

2 oz margarita mix

Lime Wedge

Put 1 ¾ oz Blackberry Moonshine in small tin shaker, add 2 oz margarita mix, add a lime wedge, muddle together, fill with ice. Shake vigorously until the outside of the shaker frosts, pour into a rocks glass. Garnish with 3 blackberries.

Ozark Distillery Butterscotch Moonshine

ADULT HARRY POTTER BUTTERBEER

Enter the wizarding world with a delicious version of Harry Potter's classic butterbeer. This "Harry Potter Butterbeer for Adults" combines the lovely flavors of Ozark Distillery's Butterscotch Moonshine with the creamy deliciousness of cream soda. It is the perfect magical elixir for adult wizards!

1 ½ oz Ozark Distillery Butterscotch Moonshine

5 oz Cream Soda

Fill rocks glass with ice. Add Butterscotch Moonshine and cream soda.

OZARK SUNRISE

A tasty and colorful beverage that perfectly embodies the essence of an Ozark sunrise appropriately named the Ozark Sunrise. This drink is like a blast of sunshine in a glass, thanks to the rich, buttery aromas of Ozark Distillery's butterscotch moonshine, the pop of margarita mix, and the bright sweetness of orange juice.

1 ½ oz Ozark Distillery Butterscotch Moonshine

1 oz Margarita mix

2 oz Orange Juice

Fill a rocks glass with ice, add Butterscotch moonshine, Margarita mix, and orange juice. Garnish with an orange wheel.

TROPICAL OD MIMOSA

The Tropical OD Mimosa blends the bright, acidic notes of orange juice with the sweet, buttery flavors of Ozark Distillery Butterscotch Moonshine to create a wonderful and refreshing beverage. Drinking this tropically inspired beverage is the ideal way to satisfy your cravings for a taste of the tropics with a distinctive twist on a sunny day

1 ½ oz Ozark Distillery Butterscotch Moonshine

5 oz Orange juice

Fill a rocks glass with ice. Add Butterscotch Moonshine and orange juice. Garnish with an orange wheel.

OZARK DISTILLERY CINNAMON MOONSHINE

CINNAMON ROLL

A delicious and sweet concoction. The creamy effervescence of cream soda and Ozark Distillery's Cinnamon Moonshine's warm, spicy notes blend to make this drink feel like you're sipping on a liquid cinnamon roll. Perfect for a cozy evening or when you start craving that soft, fluffy cake taste in a glass. Excellent dessert drink!

1 ½ oz Ozark Distillery Cinnamon Moonshine

5 oz Cream Soda

Fill rocks glass with ice, add Cinnamon Moonshine and cream soda.

CINNARITA

The Cinnarita is a spicy version of the classic margarita, mixed with the spicy and warm flavors of Ozark Distillery's Cinnamon Moonshine. The end result is an exotic masterpiece that you'll enjoy. Simple to make, it's the perfect way to up your margarita game!

1 ¾ oz Ozark Distillery Cinnamon Moonshine

2 oz margarita mix

Lime Wedge

Put 1 ¾ oz Blackberry Moonshine in small tin shaker, add 2 oz margarita mix, add a lime wedge, muddle together, fill with ice. Shake vigorously until the outside of the shaker frosts, pour into a rocks glass.

CINFUL

The Cinful cocktail is a delicious blend of rich, warm cinnamon spices and sweet tropical notes of pineapple juice. Ozark Distillery's Cinnamon Moonshine adds a spicy kick to this refreshing drink, making it perfect to drink when you want a little spice and sweetness in your glass. Cheers to a Cinful experience!

1 ½ oz Ozark Distillery Cinnamon Moonshine

5 oz Pineapple Juice

Fill rocks glass with ice. Add Cinnamon Moonshine and pineapple juice.

Ozark Distillery Sweet Tea Moonshine

OZARK TEA

The Ozark Tea Cocktail is a sweet and refreshing blend of Ozark Distillery Moonshine Sweet Tea with the tropical goodness of pineapple and a splash of orange juice. This drink combines the classic flavors of sweet tea with a tropical twist, making it perfect for sipping on a sunny day or when you're craving a delicious and refreshing libation. Greetings from the front porch!

1 ½ oz Ozark Distillery Sweet Tea Moonshine

3 oz Pineapple juice

Splash of Orange juice

Fill rocks glass with ice. Sweet Tea Moonshine, orange juice and pineapple juice. Garnish with an orange wheel.

JOHN DALY

The John Daly Cocktail is a refreshing, lightly spiced drink that combines the rich flavors of Ozark Distillery's Sweet Tea Moonshine with the spicy notes of lemonade. Named after the legendary golfer, this drink offers a delicious twist on the Arnold Palmer classic. Whether you're enjoying a round of golf or simply looking for a refreshing and satisfying drink, the John Daly is an ideal choice for getting a hole in one.

1 ½ oz Ozark Distillery Sweet Tea Moonshine

5 oz Lemonade

Fill rocks glass with ice. Add Sweet Tea Moonshine and lemonade. Garnish with a lemon wheel.

Ozark Distillery Vanilla Bean Moonshine

OZARK MULE

Ozark Mule is a delicious and refreshing cocktail that combines the sweet and comforting notes of Ozark Distillery's Vanilla Bean Moonshine with the spicy touch of ginger beer. With the addition of lime wedges, this drink offers a perfect balance of flavors that are both mouth-watering and satisfying. This is a splendid choice for those looking for a twist on the classic Moscow Mule. A crisp Summertime favorite!

1 ½ oz Ozark Distillery Vanilla Bean Moonshine

5 oz Ginger Beer (We prefer Gosling)

2 Lime wedges

Add limes and Vanilla Bean Moonshine to rocks glass. Muddle. Fill a rocks glass with ice and ginger beer.

ROOTBEER FLOAT

Root Beer Float is a delicious, nostalgic drink that combines the smooth, comforting flavors of Ozark Distillery's Vanilla Moonshine with the classic fizz of root beer. This drink puts a grown-up twist on the beloved childhood treat, offering a hint of vanilla in every sip. It's perfect for reliving good memories or creating new ones!

1 ½ oz Ozark Distillery Vanilla Bean Moonshine

5 oz Rootbeer

Fill rocks glass with ice. Add Vanilla Bean Moonshine and Rootbeer.

OZARK DISTILLERY PEACH MOONSHINE

PEACH MARGARITA

The Peach Margarita is a delicious and fruity version of the classic margarita. This cocktail combines the sweet, juicy notes of Ozark Distillery's Peach Moonshine with the tangy flavor of margarita mix, creating a refreshing and satisfying cocktail. Whether you're enjoying a summer day by the pool or out on the boat enjoying the lake, this cocktail is the perfect choice.

1 ¾ oz Ozark Distillery Peach Moonshine

2 oz Margarita Mix

Muddle peach slices in tin shaker. Add Moonshine and Margarita Mix. Fill shaker with Ice. Shake vigorously til shaker frosts. Pour in rocks glass.

PEACHES 'N CREAM

The Peaches 'N Cream Cocktail is a delicious, creamy libation that combines the sweet, juicy flavors of Ozark Distillery's Peach Moonshine with the rich creamy fizz of cream soda. This drink is reminiscent of a summer treat and offers a refreshing and satisfying experience.

1 ½ oz Ozark Distillery Peach Moonshine

5 oz Cream Soda

Fill rocks glass with ice, add Peach Moonshine and cream soda.

PEACHY KEEN

The Peachy Keen Cocktail is a delicious cocktail that combines the sweet and juicy flavors of Ozark Distillery's Peach Moonshine with the spicy notes of cranberry juice and a touch of Sprite. This drink strikes a perfect balance between sweet and sour, creating a refreshing and satisfying experience. Whether you're lounging on a sunny day or need a dose of peachy deliciousness, this cocktail is the perfect choice.

1 ½ oz Ozark Distillery Peach Moonshine

3 oz Cranberry Juice

2 oz Sprite

Fill rocks glass with ice. Add Peach Moonshine, cranberry juice and sprite.

OZARK DISTILLERY SALTED CARAMEL

CREAM CARAMEL

The Cream Caramel Cocktail is a decadent, creamy libation that combines the rich, velvety notes of Ozark Distillery Salted Caramel Moonshine with the rich flavor of cream soda. Wonderful desert cocktail or a nice nightcap to an evening on the town.

1 ½ oz Ozark Distillery Salted Caramel Moonshine

5 oz Cream Soda

Fill rocks glass with ice, add Salted Caramel Moonshine and cream soda.

CARAMEL OLD FASHIONED

The Caramel Old Fashioned is a rich variation on the classic Old Fashioned cocktail. This drink combines the bold, velvety flavors of Ozark Distillery's Salted Caramel Moonshine with the aromatic notes of orange bitters, fresh orange peel and maple syrup. It's the perfect choice for those who enjoy a timeless drink with a gourmet touch of caramel.

2 oz Ozark Distillery Salted Caramel Moonshine

2 dashes Orange Bitters

Orange Peel

2 teaspoons Maple Syrup

In rocks glass, add 2 oz Salted Caramel moonshine, Bitters, Maple Syrup. Twist orange peel over glass then rim glass with peel and drop in glass. Add ice and stir for 30 sec. Top with a cherry.

OZARK DISTILLERY COCONUT CREAM PIE MOONSHINE

LIME IN THE COCONUT

The Lime in the Coconut Cocktail is a creamy tropical delight that harmonizes the delicious, sweet notes of Ozark Distillery Moonshine Coconut Cream Pie with the tangy flavor of margarita mix and a touch of coconut cream. This drink transports you to a paradise island and offers you a refreshing experience to enjoy. Whether you're lounging on a sunny day or looking for a taste of the tropics, this cocktail is the perfect choice.

1 ½ oz Ozark Distillery Coconut Cream Pie Moonshine

2 oz Margarita Mix

1 Tablespoon Cream of Coconut

In small tin shaker add 1 Tablespoon of Cream Coconut. Add Coconut Cream Pie Moonshine and Margarita Mix. Fill shaker with ice. Shake vigorously til shaker frosts. Pour in rocks glass. Garnish with Lime.

COCONUT CRÈME BRULE

The Coconut Crème Brûlé Cocktail is a creamy, delicious cocktail that combines the smooth, velvety flavors of Ozark Distillery's Moonshine Coconut Cream Pie with the rich essence of coconut cream and the effervescence of cream soda. This drink is reminiscent of a classic dessert and offers a comforting and indulgent experience. Whether you're looking for a delicious treat for a cozy evening or just want a touch of coconut luxury, this cocktail fills the order!

1 ½ oz Ozark Distillery Coconut Cream Pie Moonshine

2 teaspoon Cream of Coconut

5 oz Cream Soda

Add 2 teaspoons of Cream of Coconut to rocks glass. Add Moonshine. Stir til mixed. Add Ice and Cream Soda.

TROPICAL SERENADE

The Tropical Serenade Cocktail is a harmonious tropical mix that combines the sweet, velvety notes of Ozark Distillery Moonshine, Coconut Cream Pie with coconut cream, the tropical flavor of pineapple juice, and orange juice. Its smooth texture and exotic flavors will tantalize your taste buds, making every moment feel like a tropical getaway.

1 ½ oz Ozark Distillery Coconut Cream Pie Moonshine

2 teaspoons Cream Coconut

3 oz Pineapple Juice

Splash of Orange Juice

Add Coconut Cream Pie Moonshine, cream of coconut, pineapple juice and orange juice to tin shaker. Fill glass with ice. Shake vigorously til shaker frosts. Pour in rocks glass. Garnish with an orange wheel.

OZARK DISTILLERY BOURBON WHISKEY

OLD FASHIONED

The Old Fashioned is a classic cocktail that exemplifies the simplicity and timelessness of a well-crafted libation. Made with Ozark Distillery Bourbon Whiskey, aromatic bitters, a touch of maple syrup, and garnished with orange peel and a cherry, this cocktail is a true classic with a delicious twist. Whether you're a seasoned cocktail lover or new to the world of mixology, the Old Fashioned is the perfect choice for savoring the rich, smooth flavors of Ozark Distillery Bourbon!

2 oz Ozark Distillery Bourbon Whiskey

3 Dashes Bitters

2 tsp Maple Syrup

1 Orange Peel

1 Cherry

In rocks glass, add 2 oz Bourbon, Bitters, Maple Syrup. Twist orange peel over glass then rim glass with peel and drop in glass. Add ice and stir for 30 sec. Top with cherry.

OZARK DISTILLERY VODKA

OZARK DISTILLERY BLOODY MARY

The Ozark Distillery Bloody Mary is a classic, flavorful cocktail that combines the sweet, crisp notes of Ozark Distillery Vodka with the complex flavors of Ozark Distillery Bloody Mary Mix. This cocktail is perfect for brunch, a lazy weekend, or anytime you're craving a bold and flavorful cocktail Accompanied by a skewer of cheese, pepperoni, black olives, green olives, pickle and a crunchy celery stalk, it is a tasty and satisfying option.

1 ¾ oz Ozark Distillery Vodka

5 oz Ozark Distillery Bloody Mary Mix (Regular or Spicy)

Skewer of Cheese, Pepperoni, Black Olive, Green Olive, Dill Pickle

Celery Stalk

Use a small tin shaker add 1 ¾ oz Vodka and Bloody Mary Mix. Fill with ice. Roll mixture between the 2 shakers until the shaker frosts up, pour into a pint glass, top with a skewer and a piece of celery.

OZARK DISTILLERY HOLIDAY CHEER

One of the specialty drinks we make at home for family around Christmas time is our Holiday Cheer. Perfect for yuletide gatherings or cozying up by the fireplace, this cocktail is your ticket to a merry and bright celebration. Raise a toast to the magic of the season and let every sip wrap you in the warmth of Christmas memories.

3 eggs whipped

1 can sweetened condensed milk

fill can with heavy cream and add

1 cup vanilla bean moonshine

1 teaspoon cinnamon

1 teaspoon nutmeg

Continue to stir in mixer until all ingredients are incorporated.

You have arrived at the section of the book where we dive into all the creative ways we have found to use Ozark Distillery products in everyday recipes. Perfect for those who believe that cooking should be as much about fun as flavor. Grab your apron, turn the page, and get ready for some kitchen fun! Because sometimes, the food fights back!

We start with Ozark Distillery Bourbon Whiskey. These recipes should offer a good variety of savory and sweet dishes that showcase the unique flavors of our Bourbon Whiskey. Enjoy experimenting with them in your kitchen!

OZARK DISTILLERY BOURBON WHISKEY GLAZED CARROTS

Discover the wonderful flavors of our Bourbon Whiskey Glazed Carrot recipe. Each bite melds the earthy richness of tenderly roasted carrots with the rich flavors of Ozark Distillery Bourbon Whiskey. This carrot glaze recipe, kissed with a hint of brown sugar, caramelizes beautifully to offer a perfect balance of sweetness, warmth, and complexity.

Ingredients:

- 4 cups sliced carrots

- 3 tablespoons butter

- 1/4 cup brown sugar

- 1/4 cup Ozark Distillery Bourbon Whiskey

- Salt & pepper to taste

Instructions:

1. In a skillet, melt the butter over medium heat. Add carrots.
2. Cook until slightly tender.
3. Add brown sugar and bourbon to the pan.
4. Simmer until carrots are well-coated and the sauce has thickened.
5. Season with salt and pepper.

Ozark Distillery Bourbon Pecan Pie

Savor the fusion of Southern comfort and gourmet flair with our Bourbon Whiskey Pecan Pie. Each slice beckons with the rich, nutty decadence of golden pecans, harmoniously complemented by the deep, rich flavors of Ozark Distillery Bourbon Whiskey. Cradled in a buttery crust and kissed with a caramelized finish, this pie is a dance of textures and flavors, promising an experience that's both familiar and exhilaratingly new. It's more than a dessert—it's an ode to the art of baking, where tradition meets innovation.

Ingredients:

- 1 pie crust

- 1 cup pecan halves

- 3 large eggs

- 1 cup sugar

- 1/2 cup dark corn syrup

- 3 tablespoons melted butter

- 2 tablespoons Ozark Distillery Bourbon Whiskey

- 1 teaspoon vanilla extract

Instructions:

1. Preheat oven to 350°F (175°C).
2. Place pie crust in a pie dish.
3. In a bowl, mix eggs, sugar, corn syrup, butter, bourbon, and vanilla.
4. Pour the filling into the pie crust.
5. Top with pecans.
6. Bake for 45-50 minutes or until set. Allow to cool before serving.

David Jr's Crockpot Shredded Chicken

Dive into a world of smoky flavors and tender textures with our BBQ Shredded Chicken Crockpot recipe. This dish marries the deep, rich notes of barbecue with the effortless magic of slow cooking, resulting in chicken that's beautifully moist and infused with every savory nuance of our Ozark Distillery BBQ Sauce. Simply set your crockpot, and let time do its magic. As the hours pass, your home will be filled with the irresistible aroma of slow-cooked BBQ, promising a feast that's both heartwarming and tantalizing. Perfect for family gatherings, game nights, or any occasion that calls for comfort food, this recipe guarantees a mouthwatering masterpiece that will have everyone asking for seconds. David Huffman Jr.

Ingredients:

- 2 lb chicken breasts

- 2 cups Ozark Distillery BBQ Sauce

- 1/4 cup apple cider vinegar

- 1/4 cup brown sugar

- 1 tsp crushed red pepper flakes

- Salt & pepper to taste

Instructions:

1. Place chicken in crock pot
2. Combine remaining ingredients and pour over chicken
3. Cook on low heat for 6 hours or until done.
4. Remove and debone chicken.
5. Shred chicken and enjoy.

OZARK DISTILLERY BOURBON APPLE CRISP

This dessert marries the sweet, tart notes of freshly harvested apples with the rich depth of Ozark Distillery Bourbon Whiskey, creating flavors that dance on your palate. Each bite reveals layers of buttery crumble, kissed with hints of cinnamon and nutmeg, enveloping the bourbon-infused apple filling in a golden embrace. It's the perfect union of comfort and elegance, a dessert that's both heartwarming and refined. Whether you're hosting a lavish dinner party or enjoying a cozy evening by the fireside, our Bourbon Apple Crisp promises an unforgettable taste sensation.

Ingredients:

- 6 cups sliced and peeled apples

- 1/4 cup Ozark Distillery Bourbon Whiskey

- 3/4 cup granulated sugar

- 1 teaspoon cinnamon

- 1/2 teaspoon nutmeg

- Crumble Topping: 1 cup old-fashioned oats, 1/2 cup brown sugar, 1/2 cup flour, 1/2 cup cold butter (cubed)

Instructions:

1. Preheat oven to 350°F (175°C).
2. Toss apples with bourbon, granulated sugar, cinnamon, and nutmeg.
3. Pour into a greased baking dish.
4. For the topping, combine oats, brown sugar, and flour. Cut in butter until crumbly.
5. Sprinkle over the apple mixture.
6. Bake for 45-50 minutes or until the top is golden brown and apples are tender.

OZARK DISTILLERY BOURBON CHOCOLATE TRUFFLES

Bourbon Chocolate Truffles. Each bite is a velvety rendezvous of rich cocoa and the rich undertones of Ozark Distillery Bourbon, melding in a seductive dance of flavors. It's not just a treat—it's an experience, where the warmth of bourbon meets the depth of dark chocolate, promising a journey of decadence.

Ingredients:

- 8 oz dark chocolate, finely chopped

- 1/2 cup heavy cream

- 2 tablespoons Ozark Distillery Bourbon Whiskey

- 1/2 teaspoon vanilla extract

- Cocoa powder for dusting

Instructions:

1. Place the chopped chocolate in a heatproof bowl.
2. In a small saucepan, heat the heavy cream until it's just about to boil.
3. Pour the hot cream over the chocolate. Let it sit for a minute, then stir until the chocolate is fully melted and the mixture is smooth.
4. Stir in the bourbon and vanilla extract.
5. Cover the bowl with plastic wrap and refrigerate for at least 3 hours or until the mixture is firm.
6. Using a spoon or a melon baller, scoop out balls of the chocolate mixture and roll them into smooth spheres.
7. Roll each truffle in cocoa powder to coat.
8. Store in an airtight container in the refrigerator.

OZARK DISTILLERY BOURBON WHISKEY PUNCH

Our Bourbon Whiskey Punch is a wonderful blend of bourbon, citrus, and sweet combining for a unique flavor profile sure to elevate any occasion. It's where tradition meets a splash of audacity, creating a drink that's both timeless and contemporary. Here's to sipping the spirit of celebration!

Ingredients:

- 1 cup Ozark Distillery Bourbon Whiskey

- 2 cups lemonade

- 1 cup orange juice

- 1/2 cup simple syrup

- Slices of lemon and orange for garnish

- Ice cubes

Instructions:

1. In a large pitcher, combine bourbon, lemonade, orange juice, and simple syrup. Stir well.
2. Serve over ice in glasses.
3. Garnish with slices of lemon and orange.

OZARK DISTILLERY BOURBON BACON JAM

Dive into a lush blend where the smoky richness of perfectly crisped bacon intertwines with the deep, sultry notes of Ozark Distillery Bourbon. This jam is a masterful medley of sweet, savory, and a touch of spirited kick. Perfect atop crackers, sandwiches, or even as a unique twist to your charcuterie board, it's not just a condiment—it's a conversation starter.

Ingredients:

- 1 pound bacon, chopped
- 1 large onion, finely chopped
- 4 cloves garlic, minced
- 1/2 cup Ozark Distillery Bourbon Whiskey
- 1/2 cup brown sugar
- 1/4 cup apple cider vinegar
- 1/4 cup maple syrup
- Pepper to taste

Instructions:

1. In a large skillet, cook bacon until crisp. Remove bacon and drain all but 1 tablespoon of bacon fat.
2. Add onion and garlic to the skillet and cook until onions are translucent.
3. Add bourbon, scraping the pan to deglaze and capture all the flavors.
4. Add brown sugar, vinegar, and maple syrup. Return the bacon to the skillet.
5. Simmer for 10-15 minutes or until the mixture has thickened.
6. Let it cool slightly and then transfer to a food processor. Pulse until the mixture has the consistency of a chunky jam. Season with pepper.

Ozark Distillery Bourbon Cream Sauce for Desserts

Unveil the secret to dessert perfection with our Bourbon Cream Sauce. This rich concoction marries the smooth richness of cream with the smooth flavor of Ozark Distillery Bourbon, creating a drizzle that transforms ordinary treats into gourmet masterpieces. Drizzled over desserts like bread pudding, ice cream, or apple pie it elevates every dish. Dive into dessert drama with a splash of bourbon brilliance!

Ingredients:

- 1 cup heavy cream

- 1/4 cup Ozark Distillery Bourbon Whiskey

- 3 tablespoons sugar

- 1 teaspoon vanilla extract

Instructions:

1. In a saucepan, combine all ingredients.
2. Simmer on low heat, stirring continuously, until the mixture thickens slightly.
3. Remove from heat and let it cool.
4. Serve drizzled over desserts like bread pudding, ice cream, or apple pie.

Ozark Distillery Bourbon-Infused Whipped Sweet Potatoes

This silky-smooth creation blends the natural sweetness of ripe sweet potatoes with a splash of rich Ozark Distillery Bourbon, delivering a side dish that's both comforting and exhilarating. Perfect for festive feasts or gourmet dinners, these whipped delights promise a taste journey from cozy to captivating. Experience the fusion of homestyle warmth with a touch of spirited elegance!

Ingredients:

- 3 large sweet potatoes, peeled and diced
- 3 tbsp Ozark Distillery Bourbon Whiskey
- 1/4 cup heavy cream
- 4 tbsp butter, softened
- 2 tbsp brown sugar
- Salt, to taste
- A pinch of ground cinnamon (optional)

Instructions:

1. In a pot of boiling water, cook sweet potatoes until they are fork-tender.
2. Drain the potatoes and transfer them to a large mixing bowl.
3. Add the butter, brown sugar, and bourbon to the potatoes.
4. Using an electric mixer or a potato masher, mash until smooth.
5. Mix in heavy cream until you reach the desired consistency.
6. Season with salt and a touch of cinnamon, if desired.
7. Serve warm as a side dish.

Ozark Distillery Bourbon Apple Pie

Ever wondered what happens when apples have a little too much fun at the bourbon bar? Introducing our Bourbon Apple Pie - the delicious result of tipsy apples throwing a party in a crust! This pie isn't just baked; it's infused with a splash of good times, ensuring your taste buds get a hint of mischief with every bite. Perfect for family gatherings where Aunt Mabel asks too many personal questions or those evenings you wish to giggle about pie conspiracies. Because every apple deserves a bourbon bash, and every bite should be a slice of fun. Get ready to laugh, savor, and ask for seconds!

Ingredients:

- 1 pre-made pie crust (or homemade if preferred)

- 6 cups of thinly sliced apples (preferably Granny Smith or Honeycrisp)

- 1/3 cup Ozark Distillery Bourbon Whiskey

- 1/2 cup sugar

- 2 tbsp flour

- 1 tsp ground cinnamon

- 1/4 tsp ground nutmeg

- 2 tbsp butter, cut into small pieces

Instructions:

1. Preheat oven to 425°F (220°C).
2. In a large mixing bowl, combine apples, sugar, flour, cinnamon, nutmeg, and bourbon. Toss to coat.
3. Pour the apple filling into the pie crust and dot with butter pieces.

4. Place a second pie crust or lattice on top. Crimp the edges to seal.
5. Cut small slits in the top crust to allow steam to escape.
6. Bake in the preheated oven for about 45-50 minutes, or until the crust is golden brown and the filling is bubbly.
7. Let it cool before serving.

Ozark Distillery Bourbon Chocolate Bread Pudding

Ever thought what would happen if bourbon and chocolate went on a blind date? Spoiler: It's a match made in dessert heaven! Introducing our Bourbon Chocolate Bread Pudding – where old bread gets a second shot at stardom. This ain't your grandma's bread pudding; it's been jazzed up, soaked in spirits, and is ready to cha-cha its way onto your plate. Perfect for those days when adulting gets tough, or when your chocolate cravings dial up the drama. Dive in, and let this boozy bread bonanza remind you that life's too short for boring desserts. Cheers to chocolatey, bourbon-soaked bliss!

Ingredients:

- 5 cups cubed day-old bread

- 4 eggs

- 1 1/2 cups milk

- 1/2 cup heavy cream

- 3/4 cup sugar

- 1/4 cup unsweetened cocoa powder

- 1/3 cup Ozark Distillery Bourbon Whiskey

- 1 tsp vanilla extract

- 1/2 cup chocolate chips

Instructions:

1. Preheat oven to 350°F (175°C).
2. In a large bowl, whisk together eggs, milk, cream, sugar, cocoa powder, bourbon, and vanilla extract.

3. Fold in bread cubes and chocolate chips, ensuring every piece is coated.
4. Pour the mixture into a greased baking dish.
5. Let it sit for about 15 minutes so the bread can soak up the liquid.
6. Bake for 45-50 minutes or until set.
7. Serve warm with a scoop of vanilla ice cream or a drizzle of caramel sauce.

The following recipes bring out the versatility of Ozark Distillery Vodka, whether you're in the mood for a comforting pasta dish, a refreshing cocktail, or a fun summer treat. Enjoy!

Ozark Distillery Vodka Dill Cured Salmon

When salmon meets vodka it doesn't get tipsy, it gets tasty! It's like your salmon just returned from a spa day in vodka land, refreshed, relaxed, and reeking of dill-iciousness. Perfect for brunches where your bagels need a touch of sass or evenings where your cracker screams for celebrity status. Dive into this aquatic adventure and experience fish that's been on a flavor vacation. Because why should humans have all the fun?

Ingredients:

- 1 lb fresh salmon fillet, skin on
- 3 tablespoons coarse salt
- 2 tablespoons sugar
- 1 tablespoon freshly ground black pepper
- 1 bunch fresh dill, coarsely chopped
- 1/4 cup Ozark Distillery Vodka

Instructions:

1. In a small bowl, mix together the salt, sugar, and black pepper.
2. Lay the salmon fillet on a piece of plastic wrap, skin-side down.
3. Sprinkle half of the salt mixture on the salmon.
4. Top with the chopped dill.
5. Drizzle the vodka over the dill and salmon.
6. Sprinkle the rest of the salt mixture on top.
7. Wrap the salmon tightly with the plastic wrap, ensuring it's fully enclosed.

8. Place the wrapped salmon on a tray and put another tray or dish on top. Weight it down with something heavy, like cans or bottles.
9. Refrigerate for 48 hours, flipping the salmon every 12 hours.
10. After 48 hours, remove the salmon from the fridge. Unwrap it and scrape off the dill and salt mixture.
11. Thinly slice the salmon and serve.

Ozark Distillery Creamy Vodka Mushroom Soup

Where velvety richness meets a splash of flavor, our Creamy Vodka Mushroom Soup awaits. Dive into a bowl where earthy mushrooms tango with spirited vodka, creating a culinary waltz that delights the palate. Perfect for those days when you crave comfort with a hint of adventure. It's not just soup; it's a creamy escapade in every spoonful. Get ready to ladle up luxury!

Ingredients:

- 1 lb fresh mushrooms, sliced

- 1 onion, finely diced

- 2 cloves garlic, minced

- 3 cups vegetable or chicken broth

- 1/2 cup Ozark Distillery Vodka

- 1 cup heavy cream

- 2 tablespoons olive oil

- Salt & pepper to taste

- Fresh parsley or thyme for garnish

Instructions:

1. In a large pot, heat the olive oil over medium heat. Add the onions and garlic, sautéing until translucent.
2. Add the mushrooms and cook until they release their moisture and become golden.
3. Pour in the vodka and let it simmer for about 5-7 minutes, allowing some of the alcohol to cook off.

4. Add the broth and bring the mixture to a boil. Reduce the heat and let it simmer for 15 minutes.
5. Using an immersion blender or a standard blender, puree the soup until smooth (or leave it chunky if you prefer).
6. Return the soup to the pot and stir in the heavy cream. Season with salt and pepper.
7. Serve hot, garnished with fresh parsley or thyme.

Ozark Distillery Vodka Lemon Drizzle Cake

Unleash a wave of citrusy delight with a spirited twist! Our Vodka Lemon Drizzle Cake is where zesty lemon tang meets the playful kick of vodka, crafting a dessert that's both refreshing and audacious. Perfect for those moments when you want your cake to have a little more party in every bite. Dive in and let your taste buds dance in this lemony, boozy wonderland. It's not just cake; it's a flavor fiesta!

Ingredients:

- 1 cup unsalted butter, softened

- 1 cup sugar

- 4 eggs

- 1 1/2 cups all-purpose flour

- 1 1/2 tsp baking powder

- Zest of 2 lemons

- Juice of 2 lemons

- 3 tbsp Ozark Distillery Vodka

For the drizzle:

- 1/2 cup sugar

- Juice of 1 lemon

- 2 tbsp Ozark Distillery Vodka

Instructions:

1. Preheat oven to 350°F (175°C). Grease and line a loaf tin.
2. Cream together the butter and sugar until pale and fluffy.
3. Beat in the eggs one at a time.
4. Sift in the flour and baking powder, and then fold in the lemon zest.
5. Pour the batter into the prepared tin and bake for 40-45 minutes or until a toothpick comes out clean.
6. While the cake is baking, make the drizzle by dissolving the sugar in the lemon juice and vodka in a saucepan over low heat.
7. Once the cake is done and while it's still warm, poke holes all over it using a skewer. Slowly pour the drizzle over the cake, allowing it to soak in.
8. Allow the cake to cool in the tin before transferring to a plate.

The following recipes highlight the unique flavors of Ozark Distillery Apple Pie Moonshine, making each dish special. Enjoy experimenting with them in your kitchen!

Ozark Distillery Apple Pie Moonshine Glazed Pork Chops

Moonshine Apple Pie Pork Chops is a unique and delicious dish that combines the rich, sweet, spicy flavor of apple pie with the savory goodness of bone-in pork chops. This recipe offers delicious and unexpected flavor combinations, perfect for those dinners where ordinary just won't cut it.

Ingredients:

- 4 bone-in pork chops, about 3/4-inch thick
- 1/2 cup Ozark Distillery Apple Pie Moonshine
- 1/4 cup honey
- 1/4 cup soy sauce
- 2 cloves garlic, minced
- 1 tablespoon olive oil
- Salt and pepper, to taste
- Fresh thyme or rosemary, for garnish

Instructions:

1. In a bowl, mix together the Apple Pie Moonshine, honey, soy sauce, and garlic.
2. Season pork chops with salt and pepper.
3. In a large skillet, heat olive oil over medium-high heat. Add pork chops and sear until golden, about 3-4 minutes per side.

4. Reduce the heat to medium and pour the moonshine mixture over the pork chops.
5. Let the sauce simmer and reduce by half, turning the pork chops occasionally, for about 10 minutes or until they're cooked through.
6. Serve the pork chops with the glaze drizzled on top and garnished with fresh herbs.

Ozark Distillery Apple Pie Moonshine Glazed Chicken Wings

Why did the chicken wing attend the moonshine party? To get glazed and praised! Introducing our Apple Pie Moonshine Glazed Chicken Wings - a dish so delightfully daring, even your grandma's apple pie would blush. Every wing is slathered in our sweet, apple-rich glaze with just the right hint of moonshine mischief. Perfect for those game nights when regular wings just seem too... sober. So, why settle for ordinary when you can feast on wings that have partied in an apple orchard under the moonlit sky?

Ingredients:

For the chicken wings:

-2 pounds of chicken wings

-Salt and pepper to taste

For the Moonshine Apple Pie Glaze:

-1 cup of apple pie moonshine

-1/4 cup brown sugar

-2 tablespoons of soy sauce

-2 cloves of garlic, minced

-Salt and pepper to taste

Instructions:

1. Start by making the Moonshine Apple Glaze. In a saucepan over medium heat, combine apple pie moonshine, brown sugar, soy sauce, minced garlic, salt and pepper.
2. Mix well and bring the glaze to a gentle boil. Let it boil until it thickens, about 10 to 15 minutes. Remove from heat and set aside.
3. Season the chicken wings with salt and pepper.
4. Put your chicken wings into a resealable bag or covered dish then pour half of the Moonshine Apple Pie Glaze over them.
5. Mix everything around really well so that the glaze is all around on every wing. After that seal the bag or container and put it in the fridge for two hours or overnight if you want them extra flavorful.
6. Preheat your oven to 425°F (220°C) while you wait for your chicken to marinate for its time. Then when you're ready take them out along with some foil that you'll use later to help clean up.
7. Lay down your wings in one layer on a baking sheet covered in foil for easy cleanup later on
8. Bake in the preheated oven for 45 to 50 minutes, turning the wings every 15 to 20 minutes to ensure even cooking and brushing with the remaining Moonshine Apple Pie Glaze each time.
9. The wings are ready when they are crisp and covered in a nice caramelized glaze.
10. Remove them from the oven and let them cool slightly.

Apple Pie Moonshine Braised Beef Brisket

Imagine the tender richness of beef brisket, slow-cooked to perfection, harmoniously infused with the sweet, nostalgic notes of apple pie, and elevated with the bold spirit of moonshine. Every bite is a taste tapestry, blending rustic comfort with a daring, spirited twist. Perfect for dinners that seek to surprise and impress. Let your culinary adventures be both heartwarming and exhilarating. Here's to a dish that truly celebrates the bold and the beautiful in every savory slice.

Ingredients:

- 3 lb beef brisket

- 1 cup Ozark Distillery Apple Pie Moonshine

- 2 cups beef broth

- 2 onions, sliced

- 4 cloves garlic, minced

- 2 tablespoons vegetable oil

- 2 teaspoons salt

- 1 teaspoon black pepper

- 1 teaspoon smoked paprika

Instructions:

1. Preheat your oven to 325°F (165°C).
2. Season the brisket with salt, pepper, and smoked paprika.
3. In a large oven-safe pot or Dutch oven, heat the vegetable oil over medium-high heat. Brown the brisket on both sides.
4. Remove the brisket from the pot and set it aside.

5. In the same pot, add the sliced onions and minced garlic, sautéing until softened.
6. Pour in the Apple Pie Moonshine, scraping the bottom of the pot to release any browned bits.
7. Return the brisket to the pot and add the beef broth.
8. Cover the pot and transfer it to the oven. Let it braise for about 3 hours, or until the brisket is tender.
9. Remove from the oven and slice the brisket against the grain.
10. Serve with the cooking juices drizzled on top.

Blackberry Moonshine Glazed Salmon

Imagine, if you will, a salmon so suave it swims upstream in a tuxedo. That's the kind of upscale twist we're giving our fish tonight with a blackberry moonshine glaze that's more intoxicating than Uncle Cletus at a hoedown. First, you lure that salmon into a skillet. Just a heads up, though: after a few bites, you may start humming bluegrass tunes and planning a fishing trip with a pole and a jug marked 'XXX'. It's comfort food, the kind of recipe that'll have you telling tales of the one that was too delicious to get away.

Ingredients:

- 4 salmon fillets

- 1/2 cup Ozark Distillery Blackberry Moonshine

- 1/4 cup brown sugar

- 2 tablespoons soy sauce

- 1 tablespoon Dijon mustard

- 1 tablespoon lemon juice

- Salt and pepper, to taste

- Lemon wedges and fresh blackberries, for serving

Instructions:

1. Preheat the oven to 400°F (205°C).
2. In a small saucepan, combine Blackberry Moonshine, brown sugar, soy sauce, Dijon mustard, and lemon juice. Simmer over medium heat until the mixture thickens to a glaze consistency, about 10-15 minutes.

3. Season salmon fillets with salt and pepper.
4. Place the salmon on a baking sheet lined with parchment paper or aluminum foil.
5. Brush the glaze over the salmon fillets.
6. Bake in the preheated oven for 12-15 minutes, or until the salmon easily flakes with a fork.
7. Serve with lemon wedges and fresh blackberries.

Blackberry Moonshine Chicken Skillet

Step right up and savor the rebellious spirit of the South with our bodacious Blackberry Moonshine Chicken! This ain't your grandma's Sunday dinner. It's like a hootenanny for your taste buds, with flavors so bold, you'll swear the chicken did a barrel roll in a bootlegger's secret stash. Each bite is glazed to sticky perfection, promising a finger-lickin' symphony that zings with homegrown berries and whispers of clandestine midnight runs. Perfect for your next shindig, this chicken will have your guests crowing for more — get your hands on it now and let the good times cluck!

Ingredients:

- 4 boneless, skinless chicken breasts

- 1/2 cup Ozark Distillery Blackberry Moonshine

- 1 cup fresh blackberries

- 1/2 cup chicken broth

- 1 onion, finely chopped

- 2 cloves garlic, minced

- 2 tablespoons olive oil

- Salt and pepper, to taste

- Fresh thyme leaves for garnish

Instructions:

1. In a large skillet, heat olive oil over medium-high heat.
2. Season chicken breasts with salt and pepper, then add to the skillet and brown on both sides.

3. Remove the chicken and set aside.
4. In the same skillet, add chopped onion and garlic. Sauté until softened.
5. Add the Blackberry Moonshine to the skillet, scraping up any browned bits from the bottom.
6. Add chicken broth and fresh blackberries, bringing the mixture to a simmer.
7. Return the chicken to the skillet, covering them with the sauce.
8. Reduce heat and let it simmer until the chicken is cooked through.
9. Serve hot, garnished with fresh thyme leaves.

BLACKBERRY MOONSHINE BEEF RIBS

Unleash a backyard BBQ revolution with our Blackberry Moonshine Beef Ribs! These ribs are not just a meal; they're a wild ride down flavor rapids with a splash of outlaw allure. We've taken the meatiest ribs and given them a long, luxurious soak in a blackberry moonshine marinade that'll knock your boots off. The sweet, dark berry flavors tango with a hint of fiery spirit, creating a glaze that caramelizes to perfection. Each succulent bite is a testament to the renegade joy of Southern cookin', with ribs so tender and rich, they'll fall off the bone and right into your heart. Fire up your oven or grill and bring your appetite—these Blackberry Moonshine Beef Ribs are ready to turn your next barbecue into the stuff of legends. Yeehaw and bon appétit!

Ingredients:

- 2 lb beef short ribs

- 1 cup Ozark Distillery Blackberry Moonshine

- 1/2 cup BBQ sauce

- 1/4 cup balsamic vinegar

- 2 tablespoons brown sugar

- 3 cloves garlic, minced

- Salt and pepper, to taste

Instructions:

1. Preheat the oven to 275°F (135°C).
2. Season the beef ribs with salt and pepper.

3. In a mixing bowl, combine Blackberry Moonshine, BBQ sauce, balsamic vinegar, brown sugar, and minced garlic.
4. Place the beef ribs in a baking dish and pour the moonshine mixture over them.
5. Cover the baking dish with aluminum foil.
6. Bake in the preheated oven for 2.5-3 hours or until the beef ribs are tender and fall off the bone.
7. Serve hot with the sauce drizzled on top.

Ozark Distillery Blackberry Moonshine Tiramisu

Indulge in the delectably wicked twist on an Italian classic with our Blackberry Moonshine Tiramisu. This no-holds-barred dessert layers ladyfingers that have been daringly dipped in blackberry moonshine, infusing them with a boozy zing that will make your taste buds dance the Charleston. Between these spirited sponges lies a luscious mascarpone cream, as rich and smooth as a jazz singer's croon. The tang of ripe blackberries cuts through the sweetness, each berry bursting with stories of wild nights and clandestine stills under the moonlit sky. Dusted with a fine, cocoa powder veil, this tiramisu doesn't just seduce your palate—it waltzes with it, leaving a flirtatious finish of berry and chocolate notes that linger long after the last bite. Surrender to the allure of our Blackberry Moonshine Tiramisu; it's a speakeasy in a dessert form, where every mouthful is a whispered secret of indulgence.

Ingredients:

- 1 cup heavy cream
- 1 cup mascarpone cheese
- 1/2 cup granulated sugar
- 1 teaspoon vanilla extract
- 1/2 cup Ozark Distillery Blackberry Moonshine
- 1/2 cup brewed coffee, cooled
- 24 ladyfinger biscuits
- Cocoa powder, for dusting
- Fresh blackberries, for garnish

Instructions:

1. In a mixing bowl, whip the heavy cream until stiff peaks form.
2. In another bowl, mix together the mascarpone cheese, sugar, and vanilla extract until smooth.
3. Gently fold the whipped cream into the mascarpone mixture until combined.
4. In a shallow dish, mix together the Blackberry Moonshine and cooled coffee.
5. Quickly dip each ladyfinger into the moonshine-coffee mixture, ensuring they are moist but not soggy.
6. Layer half of the dipped ladyfingers in the bottom of a serving dish.
7. Spread half of the mascarpone mixture over the ladyfingers.
8. Repeat the layers with the remaining ladyfingers and mascarpone mixture.
9. Refrigerate the tiramisu for at least 4 hours or overnight.
10. Before serving, dust the top with cocoa powder and garnish with fresh blackberries.

Ozark Distillery Blackberry Moonshine Sorbet

Dive spoon-first into a refreshingly rebellious treat with our Blackberry Moonshine Sorbet. This frosty indulgence is a bold symphony of wild, tart blackberries and a kick of genuine moonshine, creating a grown-up twist on a classic palate cleanser. Each scoop is a balance of smooth, fruity sweetness with a sly wink of spirited warmth, perfect for those sultry evenings when you're craving a dessert that's both refined and rambunctious. Enjoy a dish of our Blackberry Moonshine Sorbet and let your taste buds twirl in a dance of decadent delight.

Ingredients:

- 2 cups fresh blackberries

- 1 cup granulated sugar

- 1 cup water

- 1/3 cup Ozark Distillery Blackberry Moonshine

- Juice of 1 lemon

Instructions:

1. In a saucepan, combine sugar and water, bringing to a boil. Once the sugar is dissolved, remove from heat and allow to cool. This is your simple syrup.
2. In a blender or food processor, puree the blackberries until smooth.
3. Strain the blackberry puree through a fine-mesh sieve to remove the seeds, pressing with a spoon to get all the juice.
4. Mix the blackberry puree with the simple syrup, Blackberry Moonshine, and lemon juice.
5. Chill the mixture in the refrigerator for at least 2 hours.

6. Once chilled, churn the mixture in an ice cream maker according to the manufacturer's instructions.
7. Transfer the sorbet to a container and freeze until firm.
8. Serve in chilled bowls or glasses.

Using the rich and sweet flavors of Ozark Distillery Butterscotch Moonshine, we can create some intriguing main dishes that elevate familiar flavors. Here are three main dish recipes using our Butterscotch Moonshine:

Ozark Distillery Butterscotch Moonshine Glazed Pork Chops

Prepare your pork chops for a boozy bonanza that's saucier than a saloon singer with our Butterscotch Moonshine Glazed Pork Chops! These chops have been swimming in a butterscotch moonshine glaze that's so sinfully good, it should come with a wink and a nudge. Imagine the smoky sizzle as they hit the pan, the glaze bubbling up like the best kind of trouble at a backwoods still. With each flip, the chops get more caramelized than a cowboy's boots after a day on the range. By the time they hit your plate, they're sticky, sweet, and carrying just enough kick to make you wonder if they're packin' heat. These pork chops are like a hoedown in your mouth—each bite has your taste buds do-si-doing, two-stepping, and begging for an encore. So, grab your fork and knife—no, scratch that, just use your hands—and get ready to indulge in a taste so mischievously good, it'll have you saying, "Well butter my butt and call me a biscuit, that's some fine eatin'!"

Ingredients:

- 4 pork chops

- 1/2 cup Ozark Distillery Butterscotch Moonshine

- 1/4 cup brown sugar

- 2 tablespoons apple cider vinegar

- 2 cloves garlic, minced

- Salt and pepper, to taste

- Olive oil, for cooking

Instructions:

1.   Season the pork chops with salt and pepper.
2.   In a skillet, heat olive oil over medium-high heat. Add the pork chops and sear on both sides until browned.
3.   In a separate bowl, mix together the Butterscotch Moonshine, brown sugar, apple cider vinegar, and garlic.
4.   Pour the moonshine mixture over the pork chops.
5.   Lower the heat to medium and let the pork chops simmer until they are cooked through, turning occasionally and basting with the sauce.
6.   Serve the pork chops with the butterscotch glaze drizzled on top.

OZARK DISTILLERY BUTTERSCOTCH MOONSHINE CHICKEN AND RICE

Ladies and gents, gather 'round the dinner table for a culinary escapade that's about to whisk you away to a land where comfort food meets a cheeky splash of rebel spirit. Introducing our Butterscotch Moonshine Chicken and Rice: a dish so heartwarmingly delicious, it's like a bear hug from a Southern grandma with a secret wild side.

So, strap in your taste buds and get ready for lift-off. Our Butterscotch Moonshine Chicken and Rice is more than just a meal—it's an adventure on a plate, a comfort classic that's been given a shot of good-time gusto that'll have you tipping your hat with every bite.

Ingredients:

- 4 boneless, skinless chicken breasts
- 1 cup rice
- 2 cups chicken broth
- 1/2 cup Ozark Distillery Butterscotch Moonshine
- 1/4 cup chopped onions
- 1/4 cup chopped bell peppers
- 2 tablespoons butter
- Salt and pepper, to taste
- Fresh parsley, for garnish

Instructions:

1. Season the chicken breasts with salt and pepper.
2. In a large skillet, melt butter over medium-high heat. Add the chicken breasts and cook until browned on both sides.
3. Remove the chicken and set aside.
4. In the same skillet, add onions and bell peppers, sautéing until softened.
5. Add rice to the skillet and stir for a couple of minutes.
6. Pour in the chicken broth, Butterscotch Moonshine, and return the chicken to the skillet.
7. Reduce the heat to low, cover, and let simmer for 20-25 minutes or until the rice is cooked and the chicken is tender.
8. Garnish with fresh parsley before serving.

Ozark Distillery Butterscotch Moonshine Beef Stew

Feast your eyes—and soon your taste buds—on a stew that's been simmering at the crossroads of tradition and temptation. Our Butterscotch Moonshine Beef Stew is the culinary equivalent of a secret handshake into an exclusive club where comfort food gets a mischievously boozy twist.

Imagine tender chunks of beef, slow-cooked to perfection, each piece telling tales of smoky hearths and whispered folklore. These morsels are enveloped in a rich, velvety sauce where the down-home sweetness of butterscotch pairs with a generous pour of moonshine, delivering a warmth that'll ripple through you like a well-kept secret.

Carrots, potatoes, and onions join the mix, each vegetable soaked in the stew's golden ambrosia, turning this dish into a mosaic of flavors that's as bold as it is satisfying. This isn't just a beef stew; it's a hearty embrace from the deep South, a reminder of the joy found in a pot left to work its magic over time.

So, don your apron, ready your bowl, and prepare to ladle up a serving of our Butterscotch Moonshine Beef Stew. It's a meal that promises not just to feed the body, but to add a little spirit to your soul.

Ingredients:

- 2 lbs beef chunks, for stewing
- 3/4 cup Ozark Distillery Butterscotch Moonshine
- 3 cups beef broth
- 3 carrots, sliced
- 2 potatoes, cubed
- 1 onion, chopped

- 2 cloves garlic, minced

- 2 tablespoons tomato paste

- 1 tablespoon olive oil

- Salt and pepper, to taste

- Fresh thyme and rosemary, for seasoning

Instructions:

1. Season the beef chunks with salt and pepper.
2. In a large pot or Dutch oven, heat olive oil over medium-high heat. Brown the beef chunks in batches.
3. Remove the beef and set aside.
4. In the same pot, add onions and garlic, sautéing until translucent.
5. Add the tomato paste and cook for another 2 minutes.
6. Pour in the Butterscotch Moonshine, scraping the bottom of the pot to release any browned bits.
7. Return the beef to the pot and add the beef broth, carrots, and potatoes.
8. Season with fresh thyme and rosemary.
9. Bring to a boil, then reduce the heat to low. Cover and let the stew simmer for about 2-2.5 hours, or until the beef is tender.
10. Check for seasoning, adjusting salt and pepper as needed.
11. Serve the stew hot with crusty bread or over mashed potatoes.

Cooking Tips:

- The alcohol content in the moonshine will cook off, leaving behind the rich flavors of butterscotch. Always ensure that the dishes are cooked adequately to ensure this.

Vanilla Bean Moonshine, with its smooth and aromatic profile, can serve as a delightful ingredient in desserts, adding a unique depth and flavor. Here are three dessert recipes featuring Ozark Distillery Vanilla Bean Moonshine:

Ozark Distillery Vanilla Bean Moonshine Shrimp Scampi

Cast off on a culinary voyage where the zesty Italian seas meet the mysterious waters of moonshine distilling. Introducing our Vanilla Bean Moonshine Shrimp Scampi, a dish that sails the ocean of flavor with a flag of bold innovation flying high. In this daring rendition of a beloved classic, succulent shrimp are sautéed in a sauce that's as smooth and sultry as a Southern drawl—a sauce that owes its unique character to a generous helping of vanilla bean-infused moonshine.

The moonshine doesn't just bring the party; it serenades your shrimp with a sweet, aromatic complexity that's as unexpected as it is delightful. Bathed in butter, garlic, and a splash of this spirited elixir, each shrimp becomes a tender treasure chest of flavors, waiting to release its bounty with every bite.

Finished with a squeeze of fresh lemon and a sprinkle of herbs, this Vanilla Bean Moonshine Shrimp Scampi is not just a meal; it's a maritime romance, a symphony of flavors that dances on the palate and whispers of moonlit escapades on distant shores. Prepare to be swept away by a wave of culinary bliss that's as indulgent as it is innovative.

Ingredients:

- 1 lb large shrimp, peeled and deveined

- 1/2 cup Ozark Distillery Vanilla Bean Moonshine

- 3 cloves garlic, minced

- 1/4 cup fresh lemon juice

- 1/4 cup fresh parsley, chopped

- 1/2 cup unsalted butter

- Salt and pepper, to taste

- Cooked linguine or spaghetti, for serving

Instructions:

1. In a large skillet, melt the butter over medium heat. Add garlic and sauté until fragrant.
2. Add the shrimp to the skillet, cooking until they turn pink, about 2 minutes per side.
3. Pour in the Vanilla Bean Moonshine and lemon juice. Allow the mixture to simmer for another 3-4 minutes.
4. Season with salt and pepper, and then stir in the chopped parsley.
5. Serve the shrimp scampi over cooked linguine or spaghetti.

Ozark Distillery Vanilla Bean Moonshine Braised Chicken

Get ready to cluck your way to culinary bliss with our Vanilla Bean Moonshine Braised Chicken, where Southern comfort waltzes with gourmet flair in a dish that's so unexpectedly perfect, it could only have been conceived by a chef who's half-culinary genius, half-mad scientist, or maybe just a moonshiner. This is chicken that's been swimming in a vanilla bean moonshine bath, getting tender enough to make a bodybuilder weep sweet, boozy tears. It's like each piece of poultry soaked up every wise tale from an old-timer on a porch swing and decided to rebel against every bland bird that came before it.

But wait—there's more! As the chicken slow-braises to the point of "oh, my stars!", it absorbs an aromatic mixture that whispers sweet nothings to your senses, promising a bite that's as comforting as granny's quilts and as thrilling as a speakeasy's secret handshake. Finished with a sauce that could make even the most stoic chicken cross the road to try some, our Vanilla Bean Moonshine Braised Chicken will have you tucking in your napkin and tipping your hat to a flavor so bold, it's practically got its own zip code.

Ingredients:

- 4 bone-in, skin-on chicken thighs

- 3/4 cup Ozark Distillery Vanilla Bean Moonshine

- 1 cup chicken broth

- 1 onion, chopped

- 2 carrots, sliced

- 3 cloves garlic, minced

- 2 tablespoons olive oil

- Salt, pepper, and fresh thyme, to taste

Instructions:

1. Season chicken thighs with salt and pepper.
2. In a large skillet or Dutch oven, heat the olive oil over medium-high heat. Add the chicken thighs, skin side down, and brown on both sides.
3. Remove the chicken and set aside. In the same skillet, sauté the onion, carrots, and garlic until softened.
4. Add the Vanilla Bean Moonshine, scraping the bottom of the pan to release any browned bits.
5. Return the chicken to the skillet and add the chicken broth and thyme.
6. Cover and let simmer on low for about 30 minutes, or until the chicken is cooked through.
7. Serve with mashed potatoes or rice.

Ozark Distillery Vanilla Bean Moonshine Beef Stroganoff

Welcome to a rustic twist on a Russian classic, the Ozark Distillery Vanilla Bean Moonshine Beef Stroganoff. Here's where the heartiness of the heartland meets a dash of daring, a recipe that's as bold as the Ozark Mountains themselves.

Saddle up for tender slices of beef tenderloin or sirloin, seared to perfection and then lovingly braised in the smooth, sweet embrace of Vanilla Bean Moonshine. This isn't your Babushka's stroganoff; it's a dish that packs a punch while hitting all those creamy, comforting notes you crave. The Ozark Distillery Vanilla Bean Moonshine Beef Stroganoff is not just a meal—it's a boot-stomping, taste-bud-tantalizing experience that'll have you hollering "Yeehaw!" with every forkful.

Ingredients:

- 1 lb beef tenderloin or sirloin, thinly sliced

- 1/2 cup Ozark Distillery Vanilla Bean Moonshine

- 1 cup sour cream

- 1 onion, thinly sliced

- 1 cup mushrooms, sliced

- 2 cloves garlic, minced

- 2 cups beef broth

- 2 tablespoons all-purpose flour

- 2 tablespoons butter

- Salt and pepper, to taste

- Cooked egg noodles, for serving

Instructions:

1. In a large skillet, melt the butter over medium heat. Add the sliced beef and cook until browned. Remove and set aside.
2. In the same skillet, add the onions and mushrooms, sautéing until softened. Add the garlic and cook for another minute.
3. Sprinkle the flour over the vegetable mixture, stirring well. Slowly pour in the beef broth, Vanilla Bean Moonshine, and stir constantly until the mixture thickens.
4. Reduce the heat to low and stir in the sour cream. Return the beef to the skillet and simmer until heated through.
5. Season with salt and pepper. Serve the stroganoff over cooked egg noodles.

Ozark Distillery Vanilla Bean Moonshine Crème Brûlée

Indulge in the sultry whisper of rebellion with our Vanilla Bean Moonshine Crème Brûlée, where classic French dessert meets the wild streak of American moonshine. This is not your ordinary crème brûlée; it's a dessert that wears a leather jacket and rides a motorcycle through the rolling hills of flavor country.

Beneath a glassy, caramelized sugar crust - as shatteringly perfect as a night full of stars - lies a creamy custard that's been kissed by the essence of vanilla beans and the spirited allure of moonshine. The moonshine isn't just there to raise eyebrows; it mingles with the vanilla to create a symphony of sweet and smooth with just a hint of mischief, the kind that whispers sweet nothings to your palate and leaves a warm, memorable glow in its wake.

With every spoonful of this Vanilla Bean Moonshine Crème Brûlée, expect a taste of elegance with a wink of the wild side, a dessert that's as much a conversation starter as it is a satisfying finale to a fine meal. Go ahead, crack the top with your spoon, dive into the forbidden fusion of flavors, and let this culinary adventure lead you to where fine dining gets a playful punch of bootlegger's bravado.

Ingredients:

- 2 cups heavy cream

- 5 large egg yolks

- 1/2 cup granulated sugar, plus extra for the caramelized top

- 1/4 cup Ozark Distillery Vanilla Bean Moonshine

- 1 teaspoon pure vanilla extract

Instructions:

1. Preheat the oven to 325°F (163°C).
2. In a saucepan, heat the heavy cream until it's just beginning to simmer. Remove from heat.
3. In a bowl, whisk together the egg yolks and sugar until they become pale in color.
4. Slowly pour the warm cream into the egg mixture while continuously whisking to temper the eggs.
5. Stir in the Vanilla Bean Moonshine and vanilla extract.
6. Pour the mixture into ramekins and place them in a baking dish.
7. Fill the baking dish with hot water until it reaches halfway up the sides of the ramekins.
8. Bake for 40-45 minutes, or until the center is set but still slightly wobbly.
9. Remove from the oven and let cool. Refrigerate for at least 4 hours.
10. Before serving, sprinkle a thin layer of sugar on top of each ramekin and use a torch to caramelize the sugar until it's golden and crispy.

Ozark Distillery Vanilla Bean Moonshine Panna Cotta

Ladies and gentlemen, buckle up your dessert belts and loosen your sweet tooth sockets, because I'm about to introduce you to the dessert that moonwalks on your tongue and does a backflip in your belly – the Vanilla Bean Moonshine Panna Cotta!

Picture this: a panna cotta so smooth, it makes jazz sound like a rock concert. This isn't just any old Italian grandma's secret recipe; this is what happens when Italy runs a speakeasy in the Prohibition era. We take the elegant, wobbly whisper of a traditional panna cotta and infuse it with a mischievous glug of moonshine, because why not make dessert a little rebellious?

With each spoonful, you'll ride the creamy waves of vanilla bean serenity, only to get a cheeky kick from the moonshine, reminding you that this panna cotta didn't come to play – it came to party. It's like your dessert got dressed up in a tuxedo and then decided to do the cha-cha. Yes, it's smooth; yes, it's sophisticated; but it's also got a wild side that would make your grandmother blush and ask for seconds.

Ingredients:

- 2 cups heavy cream

- 1/2 cup granulated sugar

- 1/4 cup Ozark Distillery Vanilla Bean Moonshine

- 2 1/4 teaspoons gelatin

- 1/4 cup cold water

- Fresh berries, for garnish

Instructions:

1. In a small bowl, sprinkle gelatin over the cold water and let sit for about 5 minutes to soften.
2. In a saucepan, combine the heavy cream and sugar. Heat over medium heat, stirring until the sugar dissolves.
3. Remove from heat and stir in the softened gelatin until it completely dissolves.
4. Mix in the Vanilla Bean Moonshine.
5. Pour the mixture into individual serving glasses or molds.
6. Refrigerate for at least 4 hours, or until set.
7. Serve chilled with fresh berries on top.

Ozark Distillery Vanilla Bean Moonshine Bread Pudding

Embark on a gastronomic adventure with the Vanilla Bean Moonshine Bread Pudding – where classic comfort meets a dash of daring! Each bite is a cozy hug from your favorite buttery, custard-soaked bread, laced with the luxurious specks of vanilla bean that dance through the pudding like stars in a clear night sky.

But don't let the familiar warmth fool you; there's a sly twist in the tale. This bread pudding has been kissed by moonshine, turning an old-school favorite into a dessert that tips its hat to tradition while winking at rebellion. The moonshine doesn't just show up; it arrives with a gentle hum of warmth, elevating the dish with a note of unexpected spice and a whisper of good ol' southern charm.

Perfect for those who like their sweet with a side of sassy, this Vanilla Bean Moonshine Bread Pudding is a testament to the magic that happens when down-home cooking meets a splash of spirited fun. Get ready to be comforted and surprised, all in the same spoonful.

Ingredients:

- 4 cups day-old bread, cubed (French bread or challah works well)

- 2 1/2 cups whole milk

- 1/2 cup Ozark Distillery Vanilla Bean Moonshine

- 1 cup granulated sugar

- 3 large eggs

- 1 teaspoon pure vanilla extract

- 1/2 teaspoon ground cinnamon

- 1/4 cup unsalted butter, melted

- Raisins or chopped nuts (optional)

- Whipped cream or vanilla ice cream, for serving

Instructions:

1. Preheat the oven to 350°F (175°C) and grease a baking dish.
2. Place the bread cubes in the baking dish.
3. In a mixing bowl, whisk together the milk, Vanilla Bean Moonshine, sugar, eggs, vanilla extract, and cinnamon until well combined.
4. Pour the melted butter over the bread cubes.
5. Pour the milk mixture over the bread, ensuring all the bread is soaked. If desired, sprinkle with raisins or nuts.
6. Let the bread sit for about 10 minutes to absorb the liquid.
7. Bake in the preheated oven for 45-50 minutes, or until the top is golden brown and the center is set.
8. Serve warm with whipped cream or vanilla ice cream.

Ozark Distillery Vanilla Bean Moonshine Poached Pears

Prepare to be seduced by the subtle elegance of Vanilla Bean Moonshine Poached Pears, a dessert that waltzes on the tightrope of refined taste and spirited whimsy. These are not just any pears; these are the Cinderellas of the fruit world, transformed from their humble beginnings into the belles of the ball with the help of a little vanilla-scented moonshine magic.

Each pear, poached to perfection, is a tender testament to the alchemy of simplicity and sophistication. They bathe luxuriously in a concoction where the moonshine's mischievous kick is tamed by the sultry caress of vanilla beans, resulting in a symphony of flavors so harmonious, you'll hear violins with every bite.

Forget the heavy, coma-inducing desserts of yore; this is the kind of sweet finish that leaves a whisper of spice on your palate and a flutter in your heart. The Vanilla Bean Moonshine Poached Pears are not just a dish, but an experience, one that elevates the end of your meal to a poetic realm. So, spoon in hand, prepare to dive into a dish where every mouthful is a love letter to the senses.

Ingredients:

- 4 ripe but firm pears, peeled with stems intact

- 2 cups water

- 1 cup granulated sugar

- 1/2 cup Ozark Distillery Vanilla Bean Moonshine

- 1 cinnamon stick

- Zest of 1 lemon

Instructions:

1. In a large saucepan, combine water, sugar, Vanilla Bean Moonshine, cinnamon stick, and lemon zest. Bring the mixture to a simmer over medium heat.
2. Once the sugar has dissolved, gently place the pears in the saucepan.
3. Reduce the heat to low and let the pears poach for about 20-25 minutes, or until they're tender but not mushy.
4. Remove the pears from the liquid and set them aside to cool.
5. Increase the heat to medium-high and let the poaching liquid simmer until it's reduced by half and has a syrupy consistency.
6. Remove from heat and discard the cinnamon stick.
7. Serve the pears drizzled with the reduced syrup.

OZARK DISTILLERY VANILLA BEAN MOONSHINE TIRAMISU

Imagine, if you will, the classic Italian tiramisu – that beloved symphony of coffee-dipped ladyfingers and mascarpone – but with a mischievous twinkle in its eye. Enter Vanilla Bean Moonshine Tiramisu, where tradition gets a tipsy twist!

This isn't just tiramisu; it's tiramisu with a secret. Nestled between the soft, espresso-soaked layers is a bold whisper of moonshine, infused with the exotic allure of vanilla beans. It's as if your favorite Italian dessert spent a summer vacation in the Ozark hills, coming back with stories daring enough to make your spoon blush.

Each bite is a decadent mélange of familiar comfort and exhilarating surprise. The moonshine doesn't overpower; it flirts with the dish, enhancing the depth of flavor, while the vanilla beans impart a sophisticated sweetness that lingers long after the last bite, like the memory of a thrilling summer fling.

Vanilla Bean Moonshine Tiramisu is more than a dessert. It's a conversation starter, a mood setter, a crescendo in the opera of your evening. Ready your dessert forks for a taste of indulgence that's bound to raise eyebrows and elicit encores. This is where dessert becomes an adventure.

Ingredients:

- 1 cup brewed coffee, cooled

- 1/4 cup Ozark Distillery Vanilla Bean Moonshine

- 1 cup mascarpone cheese

- 1/2 cup heavy cream

- 1/3 cup granulated sugar

- 1 teaspoon pure vanilla extract

- 1 package ladyfingers (about 24)

- Cocoa powder, for dusting

Instructions:

1. In a shallow dish, combine brewed coffee and Vanilla Bean Moonshine.
2. In a mixing bowl, beat together mascarpone, heavy cream, sugar, and vanilla extract until smooth and creamy.
3. Briefly dip each ladyfinger into the coffee-moonshine mixture, making sure not to soak them too long.
4. Arrange a layer of dipped ladyfingers at the bottom of a serving dish.
5. Spread half of the mascarpone mixture over the ladyfingers.
6. Repeat the layers with the remaining ladyfingers and mascarpone mixture.
7. Refrigerate for at least 4 hours or overnight.
8. Before serving, dust the top with cocoa powder.

These recipes incorporate the unique flavor of Sweet Tea Moonshine, infusing the comforting taste of sweet tea into hearty main dishes. Enjoy your culinary journey with Ozark Distillery's distinctive touch.

Ozark Distillery Sweet Tea Moonshine Pulled Pork

Feast your senses on Sweet Tea Moonshine Pulled Pork – a dish that turns a Southern staple into a slow-cooked masterpiece steeped in nostalgia and spiked with a spirited edge. This is where the sweet, smoky whispers of barbeque meet the unexpected kick of moonshine, all mellowed by the comforting embrace of sweet tea.

This pulled pork is not just melt-in-your-mouth tender; it's a mouthful of stories – of rocking chairs on front porches, of laughter around a pit fire, and of the clandestine thrill of a moonshine run under a starlit sky. Sweet Tea Moonshine Pulled Pork is not just a dish; it's the South, served on a platter, with a side of daring.

Ingredients:

- 3 lbs pork shoulder
- 1 cup Ozark Distillery Sweet Tea Moonshine
- 1/2 cup Ozark Distillery BBQ sauce
- 1/4 cup brown sugar
- 1 tablespoon smoked paprika
- 2 teaspoons garlic powder
- Salt and pepper to taste
- Buns for serving

Instructions:

1. Mix together brown sugar, smoked paprika, garlic powder, salt, and pepper. Rub this mixture all over the pork shoulder.
2. Place the pork in a slow cooker.

3. Mix together the Sweet Tea Moonshine and barbecue sauce. Pour this over the pork.
4. Cook on low for 7-8 hours or until the pork is tender and easily shreds.
5. Once cooked, shred the pork using two forks and mix it well with the sauce in the slow cooker.
6. Serve on buns with coleslaw or your choice of toppings.

Ozark Distillery Sweet Tea Moonshine Marinated Steak

Step right up, carnivorous comrades and steak-loving savants, for the culinary curveball of the century — the Sweet Tea Moonshine Marinated Steak! Picture this: a steak so tender, you'll swear it was massaged by angels with a sense of humor. This is not just a piece of meat; it's the life of the barbecue, soaked in the South's favorite elixir, sweet tea moonshine.

Imagine your taste buds donning a pair of cowboy boots and line-dancing across a grill. The sweet tea lays down the smooth moves, whispering sweet nothings into the fibers of the beef, while the moonshine comes in with a twang, whooping things up and adding a zesty kick that'll make you want to slap your knee and declare, "Yeehaw!"

But wait, there's more! We don't just marinate this steak; we serenade it, telling it tales of grand southern soirées and moonlit shenanigans until it's infused with flavors bolder than a banjo solo at a bluegrass festival.

So fire up the grill, and prepare your fork for a hoedown, because this Sweet Tea Moonshine Marinated Steak is about to take your mouth on a joyride through flavorville, where the stoplights are always blinking yellow, and the speed limit signs are just for decoration. Get ready to cut into a steak that's soaked in tradition, magic, and a touch of mischief.

Ingredients:

- 2 ribeye or sirloin steaks

- 1 cup Ozark Distillery Sweet Tea Moonshine

- 1/4 cup soy sauce

- 2 tablespoons Worcestershire sauce

- 3 cloves garlic, minced

- 1 tablespoon brown sugar

- Salt and pepper to taste

- 2 tablespoons olive oil or butter for cooking

Instructions:

1. In a bowl, combine Sweet Tea Moonshine, soy sauce, Worcestershire sauce, minced garlic, and brown sugar.
2. Place the steaks in a resealable bag or shallow dish and pour the marinade over them. Ensure the steaks are fully submerged.
3. Refrigerate and marinate for at least 4 hours, preferably overnight.
4. Remove the steaks from the refrigerator and allow them to come to room temperature.
5. Heat olive oil or butter in a skillet over medium-high heat. Once hot, add the steaks.
6. Cook to your preferred doneness, usually about 4-5 minutes per side for medium-rare, depending on thickness.
7. Let the steaks rest for a few minutes before slicing. Serve with roasted potatoes or green beans.

These Sweet Tea Moonshine-infused desserts bring a touch of Southern charm and the distinct flavor of the moonshine to classic dishes. They're sure to be a hit at any gathering or as a special treat for yourself!

Ozark Distillery Sweet Tea Moonshine Lemon Tart

Gather round, sweet-toothed thrill-seekers and lemon lovers, for a dessert that's as sassy as it is classy — the Sweet Tea Moonshine Lemon Tart! This ain't your grandma's lemon tart, unless your grandma was known for spiking her pastries and winking at strangers.

Zingy lemon curd, so tart it'll tickle your jawline, meets its soulmate in a rebelliously sweet moonshine-infused sweet tea, all nestled in a buttery crust that's flakier than your friend who always cancels plans. It's a confectionery match made in a quirky corner of dessert heaven, where the sun is always shining, and the tea is always spiked.

Every forkful is like taking a backroad joyride in a convertible through citrus groves, with the wind in your hair and a mason jar of liquid mischief in the cup holder. This lemon tart comes with a buzz, a zest for life, and a twinkle in its crumbly eye, guaranteed to pucker your smile.

Ingredients:

- 1 pre-made pie crust (or your favorite homemade recipe)

- 4 large eggs

- 1 cup granulated sugar

- 1/2 cup fresh lemon juice

- 1/4 cup Ozark Distillery Sweet Tea Moonshine

- Zest of 2 lemons

- 1/2 cup unsalted butter, melted

- Powdered sugar, for dusting

Instructions:

1. Pre-bake the pie crust according to its instructions until it's lightly golden. Allow it to cool.
2. In a mixing bowl, whisk together the eggs, granulated sugar, lemon juice, Sweet Tea Moonshine, and lemon zest.
3. Gradually whisk in the melted butter until the mixture is smooth.
4. Pour the filling into the pre-baked pie crust.
5. Bake at 325°F (163°C) for about 20-25 minutes, or until the filling is set.
6. Remove from the oven and let it cool completely.
7. Refrigerate for at least 4 hours before serving. Dust with powdered sugar before serving.

Ozark Distillery Sweet Tea Moonshine Peach Cobbler

Sweet Tea Moonshine Peach Cobbler is the dessert that Southern grandmas whisper about when they want to feel like rebels. It's the cheeky cousin of the traditional peach cobbler that snuck out, partied with a mason jar of moonshine, and decided to spike the family recipe. Each bite is a perfect mix of 'bless your heart' and 'yee-haw,' with peaches that soaked up the sun while gossiping about the tomatoes in the next field. The sweet tea glaze is the stuff of porch-sittin' legends, giving this cobbler a drawl so thick, you'll need a spoon to help it out. Enjoy responsibly— this cobbler has been known to lead to spontaneous banjo solos and impromptu square dancing in your kitchen.

Ingredients:

- 4 cups peeled and sliced fresh peaches

- 1 cup granulated sugar

- 1/4 cup Ozark Distillery Sweet Tea Moonshine

- 1 teaspoon vanilla extract

- 1 cup all-purpose flour

- 1 teaspoon baking powder

- 1/2 teaspoon salt

- 1/2 cup milk

- 1/4 cup unsalted butter, melted

- Cinnamon sugar, for sprinkling

Instructions:

1. In a saucepan, combine peaches, half of the sugar, and Sweet Tea Moonshine. Bring to a simmer and cook for about 10 minutes. Remove from heat and stir in vanilla extract.
2. In a mixing bowl, whisk together flour, remaining sugar, baking powder, and salt. Stir in milk and melted butter to form a batter.
3. Pour the peach mixture into a greased baking dish.
4. Drop spoonfuls of the batter over the peaches.
5. Sprinkle cinnamon sugar over the top.
6. Bake at 350°F (175°C) for about 30-35 minutes, or until the top is golden brown. Serve warm with vanilla ice cream.

Ozark Distillery Sweet Tea Moonshine Pound Cake

Sweet Tea Moonshine Pound Cake is a Southern belle with a mischievous streak, all dolled up in her Sunday best with a flask tucked into her petticoats. This is not your ordinary pound cake; it's a sweet, dense confection infused with the spirit of a speakeasy and the charm of a tea party. Each slice is a buttery, golden whisper of naughtiness, soaked with the flavors of grandma's secret, a generous helping of good ol' sweet tea moonshine, giving a whole new meaning to 'tea time'. It's the perfect treat for those days when you want to indulge in a bit of scandalous deliciousness without having to don a wide-brimmed hat and lace gloves—unless, of course, you want to.

Ingredients:

1 cup (2 sticks) unsalted butter, room temperature

2 cups granulated sugar

4 large eggs

3 cups all-purpose flour

1/2 teaspoon baking powder

1/2 teaspoon baking soda

1/4 teaspoon salt

1 cup sour cream or plain yogurt

1/4 cup Ozark Distillery Sweet Tea Moonshine

1 teaspoon pure vanilla extract

Zest of 1 lemon (optional for added zing)

For the Sweet Tea Moonshine Glaze:

1 cup powdered sugar

2-3 tablespoons Ozark Distillery Sweet Tea Moonshine

Instructions:

1. Prepare the Oven and Pan: Preheat your oven to 325°F (165°C). Grease a 9x5-inch loaf pan or a bundt cake pan and lightly dust it with flour, tapping out the excess.
2. Cream Butter and Sugar: In a large mixing bowl, beat the softened butter and sugar together until the mixture is light and fluffy. This will take about 4-5 minutes with an electric mixer on medium speed.
3. Add Eggs: Incorporate the eggs one at a time into the butter and sugar mixture, making sure to beat well after each addition.
4. Dry Ingredients: In a separate bowl, whisk together the all-purpose flour, baking powder, baking soda, and salt.
5. Combine Mixtures: Gradually add the flour mixture to the butter mixture, alternating with the sour cream or yogurt. Start and end with the flour mixture. Make sure to mix just until combined to avoid over-mixing.
6. Flavor Additions: Stir in the Sweet Tea Moonshine, vanilla extract, and lemon zest (if using).
7. Pour and Bake: Transfer the cake batter to the prepared pan and smooth the top with a spatula. Place the pan in the preheated oven and bake for 60-70 minutes, or until a toothpick inserted into the center of the cake comes out clean or with a few crumbs attached.
8. Cool: Once baked, remove the cake from the oven and let it cool in the pan for about 10 minutes. After this, transfer it to a wire rack to cool completely.
9. Prepare the Glaze: While the cake is cooling, prepare the Sweet Tea Moonshine glaze. In a medium-sized mixing bowl, whisk together the powdered sugar and Sweet Tea Moonshine until smooth. You want a thick yet pourable consistency. If the glaze is too thick, you can add a bit more moonshine or a splash of milk to thin it out.

10. Glaze the Cake: Once the pound cake has completely cooled, drizzle the Sweet Tea Moonshine glaze over the top. Let the glaze set for a few minutes before slicing.
11. Serve and Enjoy: Slice the pound cake using a serrated knife and serve. This cake pairs wonderfully with a scoop of vanilla ice cream or a dollop of whipped cream.

Ozark Distillery Peach Moonshine Shrimp Skewers

Introducing Peach Moonshine Shrimp Skewers, the appetizer that decided it was high time shrimp left the cocktail party and headed to a hootenanny. These skewers have taken a dip in a marinade that's sweeter than a peach orchard at sunset and more spirited than an auctioneer with a fast tongue, thanks to a glug of good ol' peach moonshine. They're grilled to perfection, charred just enough to sing, "I've seen the light of a charcoal fire," but tender enough to melt in your mouth like butter on a hot biscuit.

Serving them up is sure to raise eyebrows and spirits alike. They're the dish that brings the kick of a mule and the sweetness of a southern summer's kiss. Be warned, though: Peach Moonshine Shrimp Skewers have been known to turn more reserved diners into porch-stompin', banjo-strummin' aficionados of the good life, one juicy, boozy bite at a time. So, string 'em up, slap 'em on the grill, and let's get this back-porch party started!

Ingredients:

- 1 lb large shrimp, peeled and deveined

- 1/4 cup Ozark Distillery Peach Moonshine

- 1/4 cup orange juice

- 1 tablespoon lime zest

- 1 tablespoon olive oil

- Salt and pepper, to taste

Instructions:

1. In a bowl, mix together the Peach Moonshine, orange juice, lime zest, olive oil, salt, and pepper.
2. Marinate the shrimp in this mixture for 20-30 minutes.
3. Thread the shrimp onto skewers.
4. Grill the skewers over medium heat for 2-3 minutes on each side or until the shrimp are pink and cooked through.
5. Serve immediately.

Ozark Distillery Peach Moonshine Baby Back Ribs

Peach Moonshine Baby Back Ribs: where the smokehouse meets the fruit stand with a detour through the distillery. These ribs are slathered in a sauce that's as sweet as a Georgia peach and as potent as your uncle's secret stash of hooch. They're slow-cooked to fall-off-the-bone perfection—a texture so tender, it's like eating a meaty cloud with a Southern drawl.

Each rib is a sticky-fingered high-five between flavor and fun, daring you to decide whether you're at a gourmet feast or the best backyard shindig of your life. You'll gnaw, smack, and lick your way to a saucy grin, with just a hint of peachy moonshine mischief in every bite. Napkins are rendered utterly useless here—embrace the mess and let the good times roll, one rib-riffic chomp at a time!

Ingredients:

- 2 lbs baby back ribs

- Salt and pepper, to taste

- 1/2 cup Ozark Distillery BBQ sauce

- 1/4 cup Ozark Distillery Peach Moonshine

- 2 tablespoons apple cider vinegar

- 1 tablespoon brown sugar

Instructions:

1. Preheat the oven to 275°F (135°C).
2. Season the ribs with salt and pepper.

3. In a bowl, mix together the BBQ sauce, Peach Moonshine, apple cider vinegar, and brown sugar.
4. Brush this mixture over the ribs.
5. Wrap the ribs in aluminum foil and bake for 2.5 to 3 hours.
6. Finish them on a grill for a smoky flavor and to caramelize the sauce.

These Cinnamon Moonshine-infused recipes offer a delightful twist to traditional dishes, adding warmth and a hint of spice to elevate your culinary offerings. Enjoy!

Ozark Distillery Cinnamon Moonshine Chili

OK folks, gather round, for I am about to unveil a recipe that's hotter than a billy goat with a blow torch and more unexpected than an armadillo at a square dance. Yes, you heard that right—we're talking about the one, the only, Cinnamon Moonshine Chili!

Now, I know what you're thinking: "Cinnamon and moonshine? In my chili?" Before you call the food police, let me assure you that this isn't your grandma's Sunday stew. This is the chili that cowboys whisper about around the campfire, the kind that's been known to cure a bad mood faster than you can say "lickety-split."

This recipe is for those who like to walk on the wild side of the culinary tracks. It's so good, it should come with its own pair of cowboy boots. The cinnamon will court your taste buds like a sweet-talking rodeo charmer, while the moonshine? Well, let's just say it'll kick things up a notch faster than a jackrabbit on a date.

So, put on your apron like a badge of honor, grab a pot big enough to feed a posse, and make sure your spice cabinet is stocked. We're about to cook up a pot of Cinnamon Moonshine Chili that's bolder than a sky without stars and more fun than a barrel of monkeys at a banjo contest.

Ingredients:

- 1 lb ground beef or turkey

- 1/2 cup Ozark Distillery Cinnamon Moonshine

- 1 can (14.5 oz) diced tomatoes

- 1 can (14.5 oz) kidney beans, drained and rinsed

- 1 onion, diced

- 2 cloves garlic, minced

- 4 tbsp chili powder

- 1 tsp cumin

- 1/2 tsp smoked paprika

- Salt and pepper, to taste

- 1 cup beef or chicken broth

- Olive oil, for sautéing

- Sour cream and shredded cheese, for serving

Instructions:

1. In a large pot or Dutch oven, heat olive oil over medium-high heat. Add onions and sauté until translucent.
2. Add the minced garlic and ground beef/turkey. Cook until the meat is browned.
3. Deglaze the pot with the Cinnamon Moonshine.
4. Stir in the chili powder, cumin, smoked paprika, salt, and pepper.
5. Add the diced tomatoes, kidney beans, and broth. Stir well.
6. Bring the mixture to a boil, then reduce to a simmer. Let it simmer for about 30 minutes, allowing the flavors to meld.
7. Adjust seasoning to taste.
8. Serve hot with a dollop of sour cream and shredded cheese on top.

Ozark Distillery Cinnamon Moonshine Stuffed Bell Peppers

Get ready to add a splash of bootlegger's bravado to your dinner table with Cinnamon Moonshine Stuffed Bell Peppers! This ain't your average stuffed pepper recipe, folks—it's a culinary shindig where the bold flavors of the South meet the classic comfort of a home-cooked meal. Each bell pepper is a colorful chariot, tender and roasted to perfection, waiting to ferry a generous filling of seasoned ground meat, rice, and a blend of herbs and spices.

But the real hootenanny begins when a nip of cinnamon moonshine joins the hoedown. The warm, aromatic spice dances through the filling, creating a symphony of sweet and savory notes, while the moonshine brings a smooth, spirited kick that'll have your taste buds two-stepping in delight.

So, don your chef's hat with a side of southern flair and let these Cinnamon Moonshine Stuffed Bell Peppers be the centerpiece of your next meal. They're a testament to the fact that when it comes to cooking, a little bit of daring makes for a whole lot of delicious!

Ingredients:

- 4 large bell peppers, any color

- 1/2 lb ground beef or turkey

- 1 cup cooked rice

- 1/4 cup Ozark Distillery Cinnamon Moonshine

- 1 can (14.5 oz) diced tomatoes, drained

- 1 onion, diced

- 2 cloves garlic, minced

- 1 tsp oregano

- Salt and pepper, to taste

- 1/4 cup grated cheese (cheddar or mozzarella)

- Olive oil, for sautéing

Instructions:

1. Preheat oven to 375°F (190°C).
2. Cut off the tops of the bell peppers and remove the seeds.
3. In a pan, heat olive oil and sauté onions until translucent. Add garlic and cook for an additional minute.
4. Add the ground meat and cook until browned.
5. Deglaze the pan with Cinnamon Moonshine.
6. Stir in the rice, diced tomatoes, oregano, salt, and pepper. Cook for a couple more minutes until everything is well combined.
7. Stuff each bell pepper with the meat and rice mixture.
8. Place the stuffed peppers in a baking dish and cover with aluminum foil.
9. Bake for 30 minutes. Remove the foil, sprinkle cheese on top of each pepper, and bake for an additional 10 minutes, or until the cheese is melted and bubbly.
10. Serve hot.

These main dish recipes make the most of the unique flavor profile of Cinnamon Moonshine, giving traditional dishes a special twist. Enjoy your culinary adventures with these delectable creations!

OZARK DISTILLERY CINNAMON MOONSHINE APPLE COBBLER

Imagine a dessert that twirls across the palate with the elegance of a Southern belle and the kick of a Wild West gunslinger—that's the Cinnamon Moonshine Apple Cobbler. It's a down-home classic with a twist, a sweet symphony of tender, cinnamon-spiced apples that have been lovingly coaxed to perfection with the mischievous warmth of moonshine.

Each spoonful is a duet of textures: the apples, soft and inviting, are tucked beneath a golden, buttery crust that's been kissed by the oven's heat. The cinnamon plays a sweet serenade throughout, a familiar tune that comforts the soul, while the moonshine murmurs a tale of hidden stills and moonlit nights, adding depth and a cheeky wink of flavor.

Perfect for a cozy night in or a grand family shindig, this Cinnamon Moonshine Apple Cobbler is not just a dessert; it's a story with every bite, a piece of culinary folklore served warm, preferably with a scoop of vanilla ice cream melting slowly on top, creating rivulets of creamy goodness that mingle with the spiced, boozy apples. Grab your spoons, y'all—this cobbler's a dessert that'll have your spirits as high as the highest apple orchard and as warm as a Ozark sunset.

Ingredients:

- 5-6 medium apples, peeled, cored, and sliced

- 1/2 cup Ozark Distillery Cinnamon Moonshine

- 3/4 cup sugar

- 1 tsp vanilla extract

- 1/2 tsp ground cinnamon

- 1 cup all-purpose flour

- 1 tsp baking powder

- 1/2 cup milk

- 4 tbsp unsalted butter, melted

Instructions:

1. Preheat your oven to 350°F (175°C).
2. In a mixing bowl, combine the sliced apples, Cinnamon Moonshine, 1/4 cup of sugar, vanilla extract, and ground cinnamon. Let it sit for about 10 minutes.
3. In another bowl, whisk together the flour, 1/2 cup of sugar, and baking powder. Then stir in the milk and melted butter to create a batter.
4. Pour the apple mixture into a baking dish.
5. Pour the batter over the apple mixture, spreading evenly.
6. Bake for 35-40 minutes or until the top is golden brown.
7. Serve warm with vanilla ice cream or whipped cream.

OZARK DISTILLERY CINNAMON MOONSHINE RICE PUDDING

Hold onto your spoons, dessert desperados and pudding pioneers, because the Wild West just galloped into your kitchen with a dessert so daring, it'll knock your boots off and tuck you into bed with a belly full of happy. Introducing the notorious outlaw of after-dinner delights: Cinnamon Moonshine Rice Pudding!

This ain't your grandma's rice pudding, no siree. It's the kind of treat that could sweet-talk a rattlesnake and charm the stars from the sky. We've taken the humble rice pudding, given it a cinnamon swagger and a moonshine makeover that'll have your taste buds line dancing in delight.

As the creamy rice simmers to soft perfection, whispers of cinnamon will waft through your kitchen like a promise of untold deliciousness. And just when you think you're merely dealing with a spoonful of comfort, the moonshine waltzes in—a smooth criminal adding a hint of rebellious spirit to this traditional treat.

So saddle up, culinary cowboys and cowgirls, because Cinnamon Moonshine Rice Pudding is the new sheriff in town, and it's laying down the law of lusciousness, one spoonful at a time.

Ingredients:

- 1 cup uncooked white rice

- 2 cups milk

- 1/4 cup Ozark Distillery Cinnamon Moonshine

- 1/3 cup sugar

- 1/4 tsp salt

- 1 egg, beaten

- 2/3 cup golden raisins

- 1 tbsp unsalted butter

- 1/2 tsp vanilla extract

- Ground cinnamon, for garnish

Instructions:

1. In a saucepan, bring 2 cups of water to a boil. Add rice and stir. Reduce heat, cover, and let it simmer for about 20 minutes.
2. In another saucepan, combine the cooked rice, milk, Cinnamon Moonshine, sugar, and salt. Cook over medium heat until thick and creamy, about 15-20 minutes.
3. Stir in the beaten egg and raisins. Cook for an additional 2 minutes.
4. Remove from heat and stir in the butter and vanilla extract.
5. Spoon the pudding into serving dishes and sprinkle with ground cinnamon.
6. Serve warm or refrigerate and serve cold.

Ozark Distillery Cinnamon Moonshine Pumpkin Pie

Imagine the autumnal hug of a classic pumpkin pie, but with a mischievous glint in its eye—meet the Cinnamon Moonshine Pumpkin Pie. This pie doesn't just sit on a windowsill; it struts down the dessert aisle with a swagger only a dash of hooch and a sprinkle of spice can bestow. The traditional velvety pumpkin custard gets a jolly jolt of warmth from a cinnamon and moonshine duo, turning each slice into a crescendo of fall flavors with a bootlegger's wink. It's a slice of the harvest with a tipsy twist, a pie that's as comfortable at the raucous Thanksgiving table as it is at a quiet, fireside feast. When the cool whispers of fall breeze drift through your kitchen, this Cinnamon Moonshine Pumpkin Pie will wrap its arms around you like a toasty flannel blanket, but watch out—it just might steal your heart and your secret stash of whipped cream, too.

Ingredients:

- 1 prepared pie crust
- 2 cups pure pumpkin puree
- 1/4 cup Ozark Distillery Cinnamon Moonshine
- 1/2 cup brown sugar
- 1/4 cup granulated sugar
- 1 tsp ground cinnamon
- 1/2 tsp ground nutmeg
- 1/4 tsp ground ginger
- 1/4 tsp ground cloves
- 2 eggs, beaten
- 1 cup heavy cream

Instructions:

1. Preheat your oven to 375°F (190°C).
2. In a large mixing bowl, combine pumpkin puree, Cinnamon Moonshine, brown sugar, granulated sugar, cinnamon, nutmeg, ginger, and cloves. Mix well.
3. Beat in the eggs, followed by the heavy cream, ensuring the mixture is smooth and well combined.
4. Pour the pumpkin mixture into the prepared pie crust.
5. Bake for 45-50 minutes or until the filling is set and a knife inserted into the center comes out clean.
6. Let the pie cool on a wire rack for at least 2 hours before serving. Serve with whipped cream, if desired.

Ozark Distillery Cinnamon Moonshine Pecan Brittle

Cinnamon Moonshine Pecan Brittle is a delectably audacious twist on a classic candy that's sure to lasso your taste buds and hold 'em hostage. Picture this: golden, caramelized sugar creating a shimmering sheet of brittle, studded with generous handfuls of pecans—those buttery, Southern darlings of the nut world—that have been roasted to a crisp, aromatic perfection.

But just as you think this brittle is merely a sweet, crunchy delight, along comes a wave of cinnamon, adding a warm, spicy whisper that echoes the nostalgia of old-fashioned candy shops and holiday festivities. And just when your senses start to settle into that familiar comfort, a cheeky splash of moonshine kicks in the saloon doors, infusing the brittle with a subtle, spirited note that's as surprising as it is satisfying.

This isn't your everyday brittle; it's a batch of sass and class in every bite, a treat for those who appreciate a spirited adventure in their snacking endeavors. Cinnamon Moonshine Pecan Brittle is a conversation-starting confection that's as ideal for gifting as it is for indulging, a sweet testament to the fact that sometimes, the most memorable moments come with a bit of a kick.

Ingredients:

- 1 cup pecans, chopped

- 1/4 cup Ozark Distillery Cinnamon Moonshine

- 1 cup granulated sugar

- 1/2 cup light corn syrup

- 1/8 tsp salt

- 2 tbsp unsalted butter

- 1 tsp baking soda

Instructions:

1. In a saucepan, toast the pecans over medium heat for about 3-4 minutes. Remove from heat and set aside.
2. In another saucepan, combine the sugar, corn syrup, Cinnamon Moonshine, and salt. Cook over medium heat, stirring constantly, until the sugar has dissolved.
3. Increase the heat to medium-high and bring the mixture to a boil. Continue boiling, without stirring, until the mixture reaches 290°F (143°C) on a candy thermometer.
4. Remove from heat and stir in the toasted pecans, butter, and baking soda.
5. Quickly pour the mixture onto a greased baking sheet, spreading it thinly.
6. Allow the brittle to cool completely before breaking it into pieces.

Each of these dessert recipes infuses traditional sweets with the spicy warmth of Cinnamon Moonshine, providing a delightful twist that's perfect for autumn evenings or cozy gatherings. Enjoy!

Absolutely, incorporating a unique BBQ sauce like Ozark Distillery's into main dishes can elevate the flavors and offer a distinct twist. Here are five main dish recipes using Ozark Distillery BBQ Sauce:

OZARK DISTILLERY BBQ PULLED PORK SANDWICHES

Succulent and smoky with a whisper of backwoods mystery, these BBQ Pulled Pork Sandwiches slathered in Ozark Distillery BBQ Sauce are a true masterpiece of pitmaster prowess. We start with pork shoulder, meticulously rubbed with a secret blend of spices, then slow-cooked until it practically falls apart with a tender glance. It's then hand-shredded, each strand soaking up the rich, smoky flavors of the grill.

But the crowning glory? A generous drenching of Ozark Distillery BBQ Sauce. This isn't just any BBQ sauce; it's a rich, complex love letter to the craft of barbecue. Crafted with the distilled spirits of the Ozarks, it offers a robust, tangy profile with a kick that lingers like a fond memory.

Piled high on a toasted bun that's soft enough to yield to the might of the meat yet sturdy enough to hold its bountiful treasure, these BBQ Pulled Pork Sandwiches promise a bite that's both comforting and invigorating. It's the kind of sandwich that doesn't just satisfy hunger; it creates an experience, turning a simple meal into a savory sojourn through the heart of American barbecue tradition.

Ingredients:

- 2 lbs pork shoulder

- Salt and pepper, to taste

- 2 cups Ozark Distillery BBQ Sauce

- 1/2 cup water

- Buns, for serving

- Coleslaw, for serving

Instructions:

1. Season the pork shoulder generously with salt and pepper.
2. Place it in a slow cooker.
3. Mix the BBQ sauce with water and pour over the pork.
4. Cook on low for 6-8 hours or until the pork is tender and can easily be shredded.
5. Shred the pork and mix well with the sauce.
6. Serve on buns with coleslaw.

Ozark Distillery BBQ Chicken Pizza

Tucked away in the rolling hills where the spirit of the Ozarks infuses every barrel, there's a pizza that's been whispering the secrets of Southern comfort into the ears of culinary adventurers. This is no ordinary pizza; it's the Ozark Distillery BBQ Pizza, a tantalizing pie that melds rustic charm with gourmet flair.

From the first glance, you know this pizza is special. The crust, thin and kissed by fire, serves as the foundation for a culinary tapestry woven with the bold, smoky notes of Ozark Distillery BBQ Sauce. This sauce, with its deep, complex layers, hints at a lineage of carefully guarded recipes and the faint, spirited zing of moonshine, giving each slice a character as rich as the distillery's history.

Atop this saucy canvas, tender morsels of slow-cooked chicken nestle comfortably, each piece a testament to the art of the slow cook. A scattering mozzarella melts into every nook and cranny, creating pockets of ooey-gooey delight, while red onions and a sprinkle of crumbled bacon add a bright contrast that cuts through the richness.

Ingredients:

- 1 pizza dough (store-bought or homemade thin crust)
- 1 /2 cup Ozark Distillery BBQ Sauce
- 1 /2 cup marinara sauce
- 1 cup cooked chicken, diced or shredded
- 1/2 red onion, thinly sliced
- 1 cup mozzarella cheese, shredded
- 1 /4 cup crumbled bacon
- Olive oil

Instructions:

1. Preheat your oven as per the pizza dough instructions.
2. Roll out your pizza dough and brush with a bit of olive oil.
3. Spread the BBQ/marinara sauce evenly over the dough.
4. Sprinkle with mozzarella cheese.
5. Scatter the cooked chicken, bacon crumbles and red onion slices on top
6. Bake until the crust is golden and the cheese is melted and bubbly.
7. Remove from oven and cut into squares.

Ozark Distillery BBQ Ribs

Step right up to the front porch of flavor because the Ozark Distillery BBQ Ribs are about to redefine your standards for meaty perfection. These aren't just ribs; they're a carnivorous celebration, a barbecue ballet danced to the tune of the Ozarks' deep, woodsy heartbeat, slathered in the kind of sauce that tells tales of secret recipes and whispers of moonshine magic.

This sauce—oh, this sauce!—is a thick, rich concoction that's sweet, tangy, and a little bit bold, just like the storied hills from which it hails. Infused with the finest whiskey, it brings a kick of authenticity and spirit to every bite, glazing the ribs in a glossy coat that's caramelized under the broiler's gentle kiss.

So, grab a stack of napkins and prepare to get gloriously messy with these Ozark Distillery BBQ Ribs. Whether it's a backyard shindig or a solo feast, each bite transports you to a world where the smoke is sweet, the laughter is loud, and the ribs are nothing short of legendary.

Ingredients:

- 2 lbs pork or beef ribs
- Salt and pepper, to taste
- 1.5 cups Ozark Distillery BBQ Sauce

Instructions:

1. Season the ribs with salt and pepper.
2. Place in a baking dish.
3. Brush generously with the BBQ sauce.
4. Cover with aluminum foil and bake at 300°F (150°C) for 2.5-3 hours or until tender.
5. Remove foil, baste again with BBQ sauce, and broil for 5-10 minutes until caramelized.

OZARK DISTILLERY BBQ MEATBALLS

When the smoky aroma of the Ozarks wafts through the kitchen, you know it's not just any meatball night—it's an Ozark Distillery BBQ Meatball event. These succulent spheres of savory goodness are a testament to the art of barbecue meeting the craft of classic comfort food, all with a twist that's as delightful as a sunset over the Ozark Mountains.

Starting with the finest ground meat, each meatball is handcrafted with a down-home blend of herbs and spices that whisper tales of Southern cookouts and family gatherings. The meat is mixed, molded, and then browned to a juicy tenderness that's as inviting as the warm Ozark hospitality.

But the true melody begins with the harmonious slathering of Ozark Distillery BBQ Sauce. This isn't just a barbecue sauce—it's a carefully concocted elixir, boasting the sweetness of molasses, a tangy zip of vinegar, and a generous helping of the distillery's bourbon whiskey, providing a robust backdrop that elevates the humble meatball to star status.

Bathed and baked in this rich, glistening sauce, the meatballs emerge from the oven sticky, caramelized, and eager to be the life of your dining table. Perfect for potlucks, ideal for impressing guests, or just a downright delicious way to spice up a weeknight dinner, these Ozark Distillery BBQ Meatballs are more than a dish—they're a bite-sized journey to the heart of American barbecue flavor.

Ingredients:

- 1 lb ground beef

- 1/2 cup breadcrumbs

- 1 egg, beaten

- Salt and pepper, to taste

- 1 cup Ozark Distillery BBQ Sauce

- 1/2 cup water

Instructions:

1. In a bowl, mix the ground beef, breadcrumbs, egg, salt, and pepper until well combined.
2. Form into small meatballs and place in a skillet.
3. In a separate bowl, mix the BBQ sauce with water and pour over the meatballs.
4. Simmer on low heat for 25-30 minutes, or until meatballs are cooked through and the sauce has thickened.
5. Serve over rice or mashed potatoes.

OZARK DISTILLERY BBQ CHICKEN TACOS WITH SLAW

Get ready to tip your hat to a new fusion favorite—Ozark Distillery BBQ Chicken Tacos with Slaw. This dish is like a backyard barbecue and a fiesta rolled into one, with each bite as thrilling as a wild ride through the rolling hills of the Ozarks.

Here's the lowdown: we start with chicken that's grilled to smoky perfection, infused with the kind of flavor that only open flames and a little patience can achieve. But hold your horses, because these aren't your average street tacos. That chicken gets a generous dousing of Ozark Distillery's signature BBQ sauce, a concoction that's sweet, smoky, and spiked with a shot of their finest moonshine, adding a rebellious zing that'll make your taste buds stand up and salute.

Now, let's taco 'bout the slaw. This isn't just a sidekick; it's the Robin to your Batman, the Sundance to your Butch. Crisp, fresh, and tangy, it cuts through the richness of the BBQ chicken like a cool breeze through those Ozark woods, offering a crunch that's as satisfying as the crackle of a bonfire.

Nestle that saucy, savory chicken and zesty slaw into a warm, soft tortilla, and you've got yourself an Ozark Distillery BBQ Chicken Taco that's more than just a meal—it's an experience. Garnish with a squeeze of lime, a sprinkle of fresh cilantro, and maybe a slice or two of jalapeño if you're feeling wild, and get ready to sink your teeth into a flavor adventure that's big on taste and bold in spirit.

Ingredients:

- 2 boneless chicken breasts

- 1 cup Ozark Distillery BBQ Sauce

- 2 cups shredded cabbage

- 1/4 cup mayonnaise

- 1 tbsp lime juice

- Salt and pepper, to taste

- 8 small tortillas

- Fresh cilantro, for garnish

- 1 avocado, sliced

Instructions:

1. Grill chicken breasts on medium-high heat, brushing with BBQ sauce, until fully cooked and slightly charred.
2. Allow chicken to rest for a few minutes, then slice or shred.
3. In a mixing bowl, combine shredded cabbage, mayonnaise, lime juice, salt, and pepper. Toss to combine.
4. Warm tortillas on the grill or stovetop.
5. Assemble tacos with a portion of chicken, slaw, avocado slices, and garnish with fresh cilantro.

OZARK DISTILLERY BBQ GLAZED SALMON

Feast your senses on the Ozark Distillery BBQ Glazed Salmon. This is not your average fish dish; it's a culinary escapade that infuses the delicate richness of salmon with a hearty soulfulness that could only be inspired by the deep, smoky flavors of the Ozarks.

Each fillet is treated like royalty, seasoned with a blend that complements the natural flavors of the salmon, enhancing but never overpowering. As the salmon grills to flaky perfection, its surface becomes the canvas for the pièce de résistance: a glaze of the famed Ozark Distillery BBQ Sauce. This sauce is the stuff of legends, a sticky, sweet-and-spicy masterpiece that boasts a hint of moonshine mystique, bringing a unique twist that ignites the palate.

The glaze caramelizes beautifully as it meets the heat, creating a glistening layer that seals in the juiciness of the salmon while adding a textural contrast that's absolutely divine. With each forkful, you're transported to a place where the smoke of the BBQ pit blends seamlessly with the freshness of the river's bounty.

Serving the Ozark Distillery BBQ Glazed Salmon is a moment of triumph, a union of land and water, of fire and finesse. It's a dish that's as perfect for an elegant dinner party as it is for a casual outdoor soirée, proving that when it comes to culinary innovation, the spirit of the Ozarks knows no bounds.

Ingredients:

- 4 salmon fillets
- 3/4 cup Ozark Distillery BBQ Sauce
- Salt and pepper, to taste
- Lemon wedges, for serving

Instructions:

1. Season salmon fillets with salt and pepper.
2. Preheat grill or oven broiler on high.
3. Place salmon fillets skin side down, brush the tops generously with BBQ sauce.
4. Grill or broil for 6-8 minutes, or until salmon flakes easily with a fork. If using a grill, you can flip halfway and brush more sauce on the other side.
5. Serve hot with lemon wedges on the side.

OZARK DISTILLERY BBQ STUFFED BAKED POTATOES

Prepare your forks for a hearty rendezvous with the Ozark Distillery BBQ Stuffed Baked Potatoes—where the humble spud is transformed into a vessel of indulgence, bursting with the rugged spirit of the Ozarks.

Each potato, chosen for its robust size and buttery flesh, is baked to fluffy perfection, with a skin that crisps up into a deliciously edible package. But the real enchantment begins when these steaming hot beauties are split open, revealing their steamy, soft insides, ready to be loaded with an array of mouthwatering fillings.

At the heart of the filling is a generous heap of pulled pork or shredded chicken, slow-cooked and smothered in the rich, nuanced Ozark Distillery BBQ Sauce. This sauce isn't just any barbecue condiment; it's a smoky symphony with a whiskey accent, adding layers of depth with its sweet, tangy, and slightly boozy notes. It soaks into the tender meat, creating a savory core that's both comforting and exhilarating.

On top of this meaty marvel, a sprinkle of sharp cheddar cheese melts into golden, gooey strands, followed by a dollop of sour cream to add a cool and tangy counterpoint to the warm richness. The final touch is a scattering of fresh chives or green onions, bringing a mild bite and a pop of color.

The Ozark Distillery BBQ Stuffed Baked Potatoes are a testament to the magic of simple ingredients combined with artisanal flair. They're not just a side dish; they're the star of the show, perfect for shaking up the dinner routine or stealing the spotlight at your next barbecue bash. Dig into this comforting creation, and let each bite transport you to a place where the barbecue reigns supreme, and every meal is a celebration of flavor.

Ingredients:

- 4 large baking potatoes

- 2 cups pulled pork or shredded chicken (cooked)

- 1 cup Ozark Distillery BBQ Sauce

- 1/2 cup sour cream

- 4 green onions, chopped

- Salt and pepper, to taste

- Shredded cheddar cheese, for garnish

Instructions:

1. Preheat oven to 400°F (200°C).
2. Prick potatoes with a fork multiple times and wrap them in foil.
3. Bake for 1 hour or until tender.
4. In a mixing bowl, combine pulled pork or chicken with BBQ sauce. Warm this mixture in a pan or microwave.
5. Slice an opening in each baked potato. Fluff the insides with a fork, season with salt and pepper.
6. Stuff each potato with the BBQ meat mixture.
7. Top with sour cream, cheddar cheese, and green onions.

Ozark Distillery BBQ Brisket Sliders

Sink your teeth into the Ozark Distillery BBQ Brisket Sliders, the bite-sized behemoths that pack a wallop of woodsy flavor in every mini morsel. Here, the low-and-slow philosophy of barbecue meets the mighty miniaturization of the slider, creating a party favorite that's as fun to eat as it is satisfying.

These sliders start with brisket that's been rubbed down simply with salt and pepper, then slow cooked until it's as tender as a folk song on a quiet mountain evening. The brisket is then bathed in the bold and boozy Ozark Distillery BBQ Sauce, an ambrosial concoction laced with a hint of locally crafted bourbon whiskey, which imbues the meat with a rich, complex flavor and a tangy kick that lingers like the last rays of a sunset over the Ozark Plateau.

Ingredients:

- 3 lbs beef brisket

- Salt and pepper, to taste

- 2 cups Ozark Distillery BBQ Sauce

- Slider buns

- Pickles, for serving

Instructions:

1. Season the brisket generously with salt and pepper.
2. Slow cook the brisket in a slow cooker or oven (at 275°F/135°C) until tender, which might take 6-8 hours.
3. Once cooked, shred the brisket and mix with BBQ sauce.
4. Serve on slider buns with pickles.

OZARK DISTILLERY BBQ VEGGIE WRAP

The Ozark Distillery BBQ Veggie Wrap is a vibrant, garden-fresh take on traditional barbecue fare that will delight even the most devoted meat lovers. It's a tribute to the versatility of vegetables when they meet the bold flavors of the Ozarks, all wrapped up in a convenient, hand-held package.

This wrap starts with a soft, pliable tortilla, ready to be loaded with an abundance of grilled vegetables. Think bell peppers, zucchini, and red onions, each slice charred to perfection, bringing out their natural sweetness and a bit of smoky goodness. There might be tender mushrooms that have soaked up the grill's essence and juicy cherry tomatoes that burst with flavor.

But the true essence of this wrap is the generous slathering of Ozark Distillery BBQ Sauce that these veggies are tossed in. This isn't your run-of-the-mill BBQ sauce. With a base that's rich and complex, a touch of sweetness, and a hint of heat — all finished with the unique twist of Ozark's whiskey — it coats the vegetables in a glossy, flavorful embrace that elevates this dish to new heights.

Finished with a sprinkle of fresh herbs, a handful of leafy greens, and perhaps a crumble of feta or goat cheese for a creamy tang, the BBQ Veggie Wrap is then rolled tight, ensuring every bite is a perfect balance of smoky, savory, and fresh flavors.

Whether you're a barbecue enthusiast looking for a lighter option or a vegetarian with a passion for bold tastes, the Ozark Distillery BBQ Veggie Wrap is a nourishing, flavorsome choice that doesn't skimp on the soulful punch of great barbecue.

Ingredients:

- 2 cups mixed vegetables (bell peppers, onions, zucchini, Summer squash)

- 1 cup Ozark Distillery BBQ Sauce

- 4 large tortilla wraps

- 1 cup lettuce, shredded

- 1/2 cup feta cheese, crumbled

Instructions:

1. Grill or sauté the mixed vegetables until tender.
2. Toss the cooked vegetables in BBQ sauce.
3. Lay out a tortilla wrap, place a portion of BBQ veggies, shredded lettuce, and feta cheese.
4. Roll up tightly and slice in half.

OZARK DISTILLERY BBQ RISOTTO WITH GRILLED SHRIMP

Ozark Distillery BBQ Risotto with Grilled Shrimp is a sumptuous culinary creation that marries the hearty, comforting textures of Italian cuisine with the smoky flavors of American Southern barbecue. This dish features a creamy risotto as its base, which is cooked to al dente perfection, each grain of rice enveloped in a rich, BBQ-infused broth that provides a sweet and tangy backdrop. Swirls of smoky BBQ sauce are artfully incorporated, ensuring that each bite offers a burst of robust flavor.

Perched atop the risotto are succulent shrimp, grilled to a slight char to accentuate their natural sweetness and lend a touch of smokiness that complements the barbecue theme. The shrimp are often marinated beforehand in a mixture of garlic, herbs, and spices to infuse them with additional flavor, and then they're grilled to perfection, offering a pleasing contrast in texture to the creamy risotto.

This dish is frequently garnished with fresh herbs like chopped parsley or chives, adding a pop of color and a bright, fresh flavor that cuts through the richness. Shavings of a sharp, aged cheese such as Parmesan may be sprinkled on top. The Ozark Distillery BBQ Risotto with Grilled Shrimp is not only a delight for the taste buds but also a visually appealing entrée, often served with a side of grilled vegetables or a light salad to round out the meal. It's a perfect example of how traditional Italian cooking can be innovatively fused with the bold tastes of American barbecue to create a truly unique and satisfying dining experience.

Ingredients:

- 1 cup Arborio rice

- 4 cups chicken or vegetable broth, warmed

- 1 small onion, finely chopped

- 2 tbsp olive oil

- 1/2 cup Ozark Distillery BBQ Sauce

- 1 lb shrimp, peeled and deveined

- Salt and pepper, to taste

- 2 tbsp fresh parsley, chopped

- 1/2 cup grated Parmesan cheese

Instructions:

1. In a pan, heat olive oil over medium heat. Add onion and sauté until translucent.
2. Add Arborio rice and toast lightly.
3. Begin adding the warmed broth one ladle at a time, stirring frequently and allowing the liquid to absorb before adding more.
4. When the rice is almost fully cooked, stir in the BBQ sauce.
5. Meanwhile, season shrimp with salt and pepper, and grill until pink and opaque.
6. Serve risotto garnished with grilled shrimp, fresh parsley, and Parmesan cheese.

Ozark Distillery BBQ Chicken & Pineapple Quesadillas

Ozark Distillery BBQ Chicken & Pineapple Quesadillas are a tantalizing fusion of classic Mexican fare with a sweet and tangy Southern twist. This dish is a creative take on the traditional quesadilla, incorporating the rich flavors of BBQ chicken and the tropical sweetness of pineapple, making for a delightful contrast in both taste and texture.

The quesadillas start with soft, flour tortillas, which are filled with tender, shredded chicken that has been slow-cooked and smothered in a signature BBQ sauce from the Ozark Distillery. This BBQ sauce likely boasts a complex flavor profile, with hints of smokiness, molasses, and a touch of vinegar sharpness—classic to the Ozark region's style.

The addition of pineapple adds an unexpected but welcome burst of juiciness and sweetness, cutting through the smoky BBQ sauce and complementing the chicken. The pineapple may be fresh or lightly grilled to intensify its flavor and add a subtle caramelized note.

Cheese is an essential component in any quesadilla, and in this dish, a generous amount of a melting cheese—perhaps a blend of Monterey Jack and cheddar—is sprinkled over the fillings, ensuring a gooey, stringy texture once melted. The quesadillas are then cooked on a griddle or skillet until the tortillas are crisped to a golden-brown hue and the cheese within has melted into a delightful, stringy web that envelops the other ingredients.

Before serving, the quesadillas might be cut into wedges and accompanied by a dollop of sour cream, a sprinkle of fresh cilantro, and a side of zesty salsa or a drizzle of extra BBQ sauce for dipping. This dish, with its combination of warm, smoky flavors and a hint of tropical sweetness, offers a mouth-watering twist on the quesadilla that is sure to be a hit with those who enjoy a hearty, flavor-packed meal with a distinctive Southern flair.

Ingredients:

- 8 tortillas

- 2 boneless chicken breasts, cooked and sliced

- 1 cup Ozark Distillery BBQ Sauce

- 1 cup shredded mozzarella cheese

- 1/2 fresh pineapple, cut into thin slices

- 1/4 cup fresh cilantro, chopped

Instructions:

1. Brush one side of each tortilla with BBQ sauce.
2. On half of the tortillas, layer slices of chicken, a few slices of pineapple, a sprinkle of mozzarella cheese, and some cilantro.
3. Top with the remaining tortillas, BBQ sauce side down.
4. Grill each quesadilla for about 3-4 minutes on each side, until crispy and cheese is melted.
5. Cut into wedges and serve.

Ozark Distillery BBQ Veggie Burger

The Ozark Distillery BBQ Veggie Burger is where the garden meets the grill and decides to throw a hoedown! This isn't just any veggie burger; it's like a farmer's market in a bun, with a license to grill. Each patty is a mosaic of vegetables, so chock-full of greens that you might feel the urge to water it rather than cook it.

Slathered in Ozark Distillery's lip-smacking BBQ sauce, which is rumored to be made with the kind of secret ingredients that could make even a seasoned pitmaster write home to mama, this burger is a smoky, saucy nod to all things barbecue. The sauce has enough tang to make your taste buds tango and enough sweetness to woo even the most skeptical carnivores.

Nestled between two buns that are as fluffy as clouds in a Bob Ross painting, the BBQ Veggie Burger is topped with a kaleidoscope of fixings: lettuce that's greener than your neighbor's envy, tomatoes so ripe they practically blush, and onions that add just enough zing without ruining your kiss-ability factor.

It's the burger that even meat-lovers might side-eye with interest, thinking, "Maybe I could swap my steak for...wait, am I really considering this?" Yes, yes, you are. Because when Ozark gets ahold of veggies, magical things happen.

Ingredients:

- 2 cups black beans, mashed

- 1/2 cup breadcrumbs

- 1 egg

- 1/4 cup Ozark Distillery BBQ Sauce, plus extra for serving

- Salt and pepper, to taste

- 4 burger buns

- Lettuce, tomato, and onions for garnish

Instructions:

1. In a bowl, mix together mashed black beans, breadcrumbs, egg, BBQ sauce, salt, and pepper.
2. Form into 4 patties.
3. Grill or pan-sear the patties until they have a nice crust on the outside.
4. Serve on burger buns with extra BBQ sauce and your choice of garnish.

Ozark Distillery BBQ Beef Tacos

Ladies and gentlemen, carnivores of all ages, prepare to have your world tac-o-ver by the sensational, the meaty, the 'I can't believe it's not a steakhouse' extravaganza—introducing the Ozark Distillery BBQ Beef Tacos!

These aren't your run-of-the-mill, Tuesday-night-panic tacos. Oh no, these are the kind of tacos that could make a grown cowboy weep with joy. Picture this: slow-cooked, pull-apart beef that's been bathing in a BBQ sauce so rich and flavorful, it could sell its own line of cologne. It's like each strand of beef won a 'Best in Show' ribbon at the County Fair of Deliciousness.

Now, imagine that beef getting cozy in a tortilla that's softer than your favorite flannel pajamas. But wait, there's more! Before you can say "Yeehaw," these tacos are jazzed up with a posse of fresh toppings. We're talking a fiesta of shredded cheese, a confetto of diced tomatoes, and shredded cabbage that's fresher than a farmer's almanac.

And let's not forget the dollop of sour cream, as cool as the other side of the pillow, ready to soothe your palate between each smoky, savory bite. The Ozark Distillery BBQ Beef Tacos are so good, they'll make you want to slap on a sombrero, grab a mariachi band, and proclaim your love for BBQ on the nearest street corner.

So, grab a napkin—or better yet, a bib, and settle down to a few Ozark Distillery BBQ Beef Taco's!

Ingredients:

- 2 lbs beef chunks or stew meat

- 1 cup Ozark Distillery BBQ Sauce

- Salt and pepper, to taste

- 8 tortillas

- 1 cup coleslaw or shredded cabbage

- 1/2 cup diced tomatoes

Instructions:

1. Season beef chunks with salt and pepper.
2. In a slow cooker, add beef and BBQ sauce. Cook on low for 6-8 hours or until meat is tender and can be easily shredded.
3. Shred the beef in the cooker and mix well with the sauce.
4. Serve on tortillas with coleslaw or shredded cabbage and diced tomatoes.

OZARK DISTILLERY BBQ PASTA SALAD

Ozark Distillery BBQ Pasta Salad takes the classic, cool comfort of a picnic pasta salad and gives it a smoky, savory twist that could only come from the deep tradition of barbecue mastery. Imagine your fork diving into a fusion of al dente pasta spirals, each twirl capturing a mix of summer veggies and a generous drizzle of that bold Ozark Distillery BBQ sauce, known for its secret blend of spices and just the right balance of tangy and sweet.

This isn't your grandma's pasta salad (unless she's been moonlighting as a pitmaster). The noodles act as a canvas for a colorful array of fresh, crunchy vegetables—think bell peppers in a traffic light of colors, cherry tomatoes as plump as a harvest moon, and red onions sharp enough to make a lumberjack sing soprano. But the true head-turner is the way the BBQ sauce clings to every nook and cranny, promising a flavor rodeo with every bite.

Then, because this is the Ozarks and they do things with a little extra flair, you might find surprises tossed into the mix—like kernels of sweet corn that pop like a banjo string or black beans that bring a down-home earthiness. And let's not forget shreds of smoked cheese that melt slightly under the sun, hugging the pasta like a warm Southern embrace.

Best served with a side of laughter and good company, Ozark Distillery BBQ Pasta Salad is the dish that doesn't just show up to the potluck—it arrives, kicks up its boots, and steals the show. It's as if the salad whispers to the burgers and hot dogs, "Move over, folks, and watch how it's done." So, slap on your sunglasses, let the ice-cold lemonade flow, and dig into a bowl of this smoky summer symphony, y'all—it's a flavor hoedown that's fixin' to be memorable.

Ingredients:

- 2 cups cooked pasta (like penne or rotini)

- 1 cup grilled vegetables (bell peppers, zucchini, onions)

- 1/2 cup Ozark Distillery BBQ Sauce

- 1/4 cup mayonnaise

- 1/2 cup corn kernels

- 1/4 cup fresh basil, chopped

- Salt and pepper, to taste

Instructions:

1. In a large bowl, combine the cooked pasta, grilled vegetables, and corn.
2. In a separate bowl, whisk together the BBQ sauce and mayonnaise.
3. Pour the sauce mixture over the pasta and vegetables, stirring to coat well.
4. Season with salt and pepper, and garnish with fresh basil.

OZARK DISTILLERY BBQ BAKED BEANS WITH BACON

Ozark Distillery BBQ Baked Beans with Bacon is a side dish that refuses to play second fiddle to any main course. It's a harmonious blend of slow-cooked, tender beans and smoky, crispy bacon, all simmered in a sauce that's got more secrets than a moonshiner's diary. This is the kind of dish that could make even a beanstalk grow a little taller just to get a whiff.

The beans themselves are a hearty variety, likely navy or pinto, that have been patiently absorbing flavors in the low and slow heat of the oven or stovetop. They take on the sweetness of molasses, the richness of brown sugar, and a tanginess courtesy of a splash of apple cider vinegar—all components of a BBQ sauce worthy of the Ozark Distillery name.

But let's talk about the bacon. Oh, the bacon! It's not just sprinkled on top as an afterthought. No, sir. It's woven throughout the dish, rendering its fat and imparting a decadent, meaty flavor that infuses every bean. It's the kind of touch that has vegetarians peeking over their salads and questioning all their life choices.

Now, picture those beans, all sticky and sweet, with a smoky undercurrent that could only come from the depths of a well-seasoned pit. Every spoonful is a little bit of Southern summer on a plate, a hickory kiss of the Ozarks that plays as well with smoked ribs as it does with a solo spoon.

So, when you scoop up a serving of Ozark Distillery BBQ Baked Beans with Bacon, you're not just getting a side dish. You're getting a spoonful of tradition, a dash of innovation, and a whole lot of flavor that's bound to make your BBQ plate feel like a feast fit for a Ozark king.

Ingredients:

- 2 cans (16 oz each) navy beans or pinto beans, drained and rinsed

- 1/2 cup Ozark Distillery BBQ Sauce

- 1/2 cup diced onions

- 4 strips of bacon, cooked and crumbled

- 2 tbsp brown sugar

- 1 tsp mustard

- Salt and pepper, to taste

Instructions:

1. Preheat oven to 350°F (175°C).
2. In a mixing bowl, combine beans, BBQ sauce, onions, crumbled bacon, brown sugar, and mustard. Season with salt and pepper.
3. Transfer the bean mixture to a baking dish.
4. Bake uncovered for 45 minutes or until bubbly and slightly caramelized on top.

Ozark Distillery BBQ Veggie Flatbread

The Ozark Distillery BBQ Veggie Flatbread is where the garden and the grill join forces for a flavor fiesta that's all dressed up on a crispy canvas. This is not your average flatbread; it's a veggie-packed masterpiece, slathered with that rich, smoky BBQ sauce that the Ozark Distillery is whispered about in hushed, hungry tones.

The foundation of this veggie spectacle is a flatbread that's the perfect combination of chewy and crispy, with edges that crunch like autumn leaves under cowboy boots. And, of course, the whole thing is generously sprinkled with a mix of melted cheeses, because in the Ozarks, even the vegetables get a cozy cheese blanket.

Served as a communal centerpiece or a personal indulgence, the Ozark Distillery BBQ Veggie Flatbread is the kind of dish that even the most devoted meat lovers might side-eye with envy. It's a flavorful reminder that in the land of BBQ, there's more than one way to steal the show— and this veggie flatbread is out here doing it with flair and fire.

Ingredients:

- 1 large flatbread or naan

- 1/2 cup Ozark Distillery BBQ Sauce

- 1 cup mixed grilled vegetables (zucchini, bell peppers, onions)

- 1/2 cup crumbled goat cheese

- 2 tbsp fresh basil, chopped

Instructions:

1. Preheat oven to 400°F (200°C).
2. Place flatbread on a baking sheet.
3. Spread BBQ sauce evenly over the flatbread.
4. Top with grilled vegetables and crumbled goat cheese.
5. Bake for 10-12 minutes or until edges are crispy.
6. Garnish with fresh basil, slice, and serve.

OZARK DISTILLERY SALTED CARAMEL MOONSHINE CHICKEN

The Ozark Distillery Salted Caramel Moonshine Chicken is a dish that boldly struts across the line between savory and sweet, and it does so with a swagger that only a chicken soaked in moonshine could possess. This is a bird that's been bathing in luxury, immersed in a marinade of Ozark's finest salted caramel moonshine, which whispers of caramelized sugar with a hint of briny defiance.

This chicken doesn't just get cooked; it gets serenaded in a skillet or roasted in the oven until its skin crisps into a golden-brown hue that could make the sun itself wear shades. Underneath that glistening exterior is the succulent, tender meat that's been kissed by the smoke and the oak of the moonshine barrel, with an undercurrent of salted caramel that gives it a flavor as rich as a gold rush.

Imagine every bite oozing with a buttery, sweet and salty goodness that dances on your palate, paired with a slight moonshine kick that's more of a friendly nudge than a boot-scootin' shove. It's like a barn dance for your taste buds, where every morsel is a two-step between classic Southern barbecue and a dessert that decided it wanted to be dinner.

And just when you think it can't get any better, this chicken is often served with a side of something equally indulgent, perhaps roasted root vegetables caramelized at the edges, or a fluffy pile of mashed potatoes that serve as the perfect moonshine sauce reservoir.

The Ozark Distillery Salted Caramel Moonshine Chicken isn't just a meal; it's a conversation starter, a centerpiece, and a way to make your dinner guests wonder if they've been transported to a place where the chicken coop is made of candy and the moon shines just a bit brighter. So, buckle up your taste buds, because this chicken is taking you on a culinary joyride through the hills of sweet, savory, and downright delicious.

Ingredients:

- 4 chicken breasts

- 1/2 cup Ozark Distillery Salted Caramel Moonshine

- 1/2 cup chicken broth

- 2 tbsp Dijon mustard

- 2 tbsp unsalted butter

- Salt and pepper, to taste

- Fresh thyme for garnish

Instructions:

1. Season chicken breasts with salt and pepper.
2. In a large skillet, melt the butter over medium-high heat. Add the chicken breasts and cook until golden on both sides.
3. In a bowl, whisk together the Salted Caramel Moonshine, chicken broth, and Dijon mustard.
4. Pour the mixture over the chicken in the skillet. Bring to a boil, then reduce heat to medium-low and simmer until the chicken is cooked through and the sauce has thickened.
5. Serve hot, garnished with fresh thyme.

OZARK DISTILLERY SALTED CARAMEL MOONSHINE BRAISED BRISKET

Introducing the dish that's destined to be the moonshine in your life, the sparkle in your smoky meat sky—the one and only Ozark Distillery Salted Caramel Moonshine Braised Brisket. This brisket has been bathed in a marinade that's so divinely boozy, it might just make the bottle of moonshine blush with modesty.

This ain't your average brisket—it's like it graduated top of its class at Barbecue University with a PhD in 'Holy Smokes'. The salted caramel moonshine does a little do-si-do with the beef, infusing it with a sweet kick that's smoother than a silk kerchief in a soft summer breeze. It's slow-cooked to the point where it practically whispers sweet nothings to your fork before falling apart at the slightest touch.

Each slice is so tender, rumor has it that the brisket sends love letters to the salted caramel moonshine, thanking it for the dance. The meat is then finished with a glaze that's sticky, sweet, and with just enough salt to make your taste buds sing a country ballad in perfect harmony.

Ozark Distillery's concoction is for those who like their meat with a side of mischief. It's the brisket that other meats gossip about, the one that shows up fashionably late to the BBQ party because, darling, perfection takes time. So, pull up a chair, tuck a napkin into your collar, and raise a glass to the brisket that's living its best life soaked in moonshine magic—just be sure not to light a match too close, or you'll have more than just a dinner show!

Ingredients:

- 3 lbs beef brisket

- 1 cup Ozark Distillery Salted Caramel Moonshine

- 2 cups beef broth

- 1 onion, thinly sliced

- 3 cloves garlic, minced

- 2 tbsp vegetable oil

- Salt and pepper, to taste

- Fresh rosemary for garnish

Instructions:

1. Preheat the oven to 300°F (150°C).
2. Season the brisket with salt and pepper.
3. Heat the vegetable oil in a large oven-proof pot or Dutch oven over medium-high heat. Add the brisket and brown on both sides.
4. Remove the brisket and set aside. In the same pot, add the onions and garlic, sautéing until translucent.
5. Add the Salted Caramel Moonshine to deglaze the pot, scraping the brown bits from the bottom.
6. Return the brisket to the pot and add the beef broth.
7. Cover and transfer the pot to the oven. Cook for about 3-4 hours or until the brisket is tender.
8. Remove from the oven and let rest for a few minutes before slicing. Serve hot, garnished with fresh rosemary.

OZARK DISTILLERY SALTED CARAMEL MOONSHINE SAUSAGE PASTA

Picture this: a pasta dish so daring, it throws caution to the wind and invites a moonshiner to the dinner table. Meet the Ozark Distillery Salted Caramel Moonshine Sausage Pasta, the culinary equivalent of a barn dance in your mouth.

In a kitchen not far from the rolling hills where moonshiners once roamed, a pot of pasta is boiling with anticipation. As it cooks to al dente perfection, it's blissfully unaware that it's about to be tangled up with a saucy concoction that's equal parts rustic and ritzy.

Enter the sizzling sausage, browned to a juicy nirvana and infused with the sweet, rebellious kick of salted caramel moonshine. Yes, you heard that right—moonshine! The sauce clings to the sausage like gossip in a small town, rich, sticky, and sweet with a hint of fun from that good ol' homemade hooch.

Tossed together, the pasta and sausage are then showered with a cascade of Parmesan cheese, which melts over them like golden sunshine on a Smoky Mountain morning. And just when you think it's safe to go back into the kitchen, a pinch of red pepper flakes is sprinkled in, adding a whisper of heat that's more surprising than finding a squirrel in your still.

This dish is not just a meal; it's a story of flavor, an ode to the Ozarks, and a testament to the fact that sometimes, the most unconventional pairings are the most delightful. Ozark Distillery Salted Caramel Moonshine Sausage Pasta—it's like a backwoods hug for your taste buds.

Ingredients:

- 8 oz pasta of your choice

- 4 sausages, sliced into rounds

- 1/2 cup Ozark Distillery Salted Caramel Moonshine

- 1/2 cup heavy cream

- 2 tbsp olive oil

- 1 onion, diced

- 2 cloves garlic, minced

- Salt and pepper, to taste

- Grated Parmesan and chopped parsley for garnish

Instructions:

1. Cook the pasta according to package instructions, then drain and set aside.
2. Heat the olive oil in a large skillet over medium heat. Add the sausages and cook until browned.
3. Remove the sausages from the skillet and set aside.
4. In the same skillet, add the onion and garlic, sautéing until translucent.
5. Pour in the Salted Caramel Moonshine, letting it simmer and reduce by half.
6. Add the heavy cream and stir to combine. Return the sausages to the skillet.
7. Add the cooked pasta to the skillet, tossing to combine with the sauce.
8. Season with salt and pepper.
9. Serve hot, garnished with grated Parmesan and chopped parsley.

OZARK DISTILLERY SALTED CARAMEL MOONSHINE APPLE PIE

Surrender to the sweet seduction of the Ozark Distillery Salted Caramel Moonshine Apple Pie, where the comforting warmth of a classic American dessert meets the rebellious spirit of the Ozarks. This isn't just a pie; it's a slice of Americana, spiked with a good-time twist that's as mischievous as it is delicious.

Beneath a flaky, golden crust lies a luscious filling of tender, spice-kissed apples, each piece swaddled in a rich, velvety sauce that sings with the notes of homemade salted caramel. But the magic doesn't stop there—the caramel is lovingly laced with Ozark Distillery's own Salted Caramel Moonshine, infusing the pie with a smooth, smoky flavor that's both unexpected and utterly delightful.

As you cut through the buttery pastry, the filling oozes out, begging to be paired with a scoop of vanilla ice cream or a dollop of whipped cream. Every bite is a harmonious dance of sweet and salty, with a kick of moonshine boldness that elevates this pie from simply homemade to downright heavenly.

Perfect for holiday feasts, family get-togethers, or just a decadent treat at the end of a meal, the Ozark Distillery Salted Caramel Moonshine Apple Pie promises a taste of the extraordinary, a pie that's as heartwarming as the Ozark hospitality and as spirited as a backwoods hoedown.

Ingredients:

- 1 pre-made pie crust (or homemade if preferred)

- 4-5 large apples, peeled, cored, and thinly sliced

- 1/2 cup Ozark Distillery Salted Caramel Moonshine

- 1/4 cup brown sugar

- 2 tsp cinnamon

- 1 tbsp cornstarch

- Pinch of salt

- 1 egg (for egg wash)

- Granulated sugar for sprinkling

Instructions:

1. Preheat the oven to 375°F (190°C).
2. Toss apple slices with brown sugar, cinnamon, cornstarch, and salt.
3. Pour in the Salted Caramel Moonshine and mix until apples are well-coated.
4. Fill the pie crust with the apple mixture.
5. Use a second pie crust or lattice strips to cover the pie.
6. Brush with beaten egg and sprinkle with granulated sugar.
7. Bake for about 50 minutes or until crust is golden brown.
8. Serve with whipped cream or ice cream.

OZARK DISTILLERY SALTED CARAMEL MOONSHINE ICE CREAM

Dive into the creamy dreaminess of Salted Caramel Moonshine Ice Cream – a dessert that's playing a deliciously dangerous game of 'sweet meets heat'. Each scoop is a velvety smooth, cold confection with a caramelized soul, laced with a daring hint of moonshine that subtly warms your palate while the artisanal salted caramel weaves in a kick of contrast that'll have your taste buds dancing on a tightrope of flavor. It's not just ice cream; it's a frosty fiesta of elegance with a backwoods wink, ready to make your freezer the coolest speakeasy in town.

Ingredients:

- 2 cups heavy cream

- 1 cup whole milk

- 3/4 cup sugar

- 1/2 cup Ozark Distillery Salted Caramel Moonshine

- Pinch of salt

Instructions:

1. Mix together heavy cream, milk, sugar, and salt until sugar is dissolved.
2. Stir in the Salted Caramel Moonshine.
3. Pour the mixture into an ice cream maker and churn according to manufacturer's instructions.
4. Transfer to an airtight container and freeze until set.
5. Serve with a drizzle of caramel sauce if desired.

Ozark Distillery Moonshine Salted Caramel Brownies

Welcome to the slightly tipsy, decadently gooey world of Salted Caramel Moonshine Brownies – the treat that parties harder than your aunt at a wedding reception! These brownies come from a place where chocolate isn't just a flavor, it's an invitation to indulge in a little kitchen mischief. We've taken the classic fudgy favorite and cranked it up a notch with a swig and swirl of salted caramel moonshine, because life is too short for boring brownies.

Each square is a mouthful of merriment, where the smooth caramel whispers sweet nothings to the bold, spirited kick of the moonshine, and the rich chocolate holds everything together like the best friend who remembers to bring the snacks to the after-party. So, buckle up your sweet tooth, because it's about to go on the most delightful joyride through Flavor Town. And yes, licking the spoon is not just recommended, it's practically a requirement!

Ingredients:

- 1 box brownie mix (or homemade brownie batter)

- 1/4 cup Ozark Distillery Salted Caramel Moonshine

- Sea salt for sprinkling

Instructions:

1. Prepare brownie batter as instructed, but substitute water (or part of it) with Salted Caramel Moonshine.
2. Pour batter into a greased baking dish.
3. Sprinkle with sea salt.
4. Bake as instructed or until a toothpick comes out clean.
5. Let cool, slice, and serve.

Ozark Distillery Salted Caramel Moonshine Crepes

Prepare to unroll the red carpet for your morning taste buds because Salted Caramel Moonshine Crepes are flipping into town and they're bringing the buzz of Hollywood with them. Picture this: delicate crepes, as thin and sophisticated as a French accent, drenched in a sinfully good salted caramel sauce that's been spiked with just enough moonshine to make your grandmother gasp and ask for seconds.

This is the breakfast of champions who thought they had tried every champion's breakfast. It's a sweet, tipsy twist on a Parisian classic that's ready to waltz onto your plate and tap dance on your tongue. So put on your fancy pants and a sprinkle of powdered sugar; it's time to indulge in a breakfast that's as decadently delightful as it is amusingly inebriating. Bon appétit, y'all!

Ingredients:

- 1 cup all-purpose flour

- 1 1/2 cups milk

- 2 eggs

- Pinch of salt

- Butter for frying

- 1/2 cup Ozark Distillery Salted Caramel Moonshine

- 1/4 cup sugar

Instructions:

1. Blend flour, milk, eggs, and salt until smooth to make the crepe batter.
2. Heat a non-stick skillet and lightly grease with butter.
3. Pour a ladle of batter into the skillet, tilting to spread it thinly.
4. Cook until golden on both sides. Repeat with remaining batter.
5. For the sauce, heat sugar in a saucepan until it melts into a caramel. Slowly add the moonshine, stirring constantly.
6. Drizzle caramel moonshine sauce over crepes and serve.

Certainly! Here are five main dish recipes using Ozark Distillery Coconut Cream Pie Moonshine:

OZARK DISTILLERY COCONUT MOONSHINE CHICKEN

Get ready to ruffle some feathers with our Coconut Moonshine Chicken, a dish that's stirring up the roost with its island-infused antics and a splash of good-time spirits! This chicken has been bathed in the creamy luxury of coconut cream pie moonshine, for a flavor that dances on the edge of daring. It's a culinary dance where tender poultry pirouettes in a sauce so sumptuously spiked, your taste buds might just start singing karaoke. This isn't just dinner; it's a tropical ticket to a plate where every bite is a sip of vacation and every forkful has a story to tell. Dive into the Coconut Moonshine Chicken, and let your palate party like it's on permanent holiday!

Ingredients:

- 4 boneless, skinless chicken breasts

- 1/2 cup Ozark Distillery Coconut Cream Pie Moonshine

- 1/2 cup coconut milk

- 2 tbsp soy sauce

- 1 tbsp brown sugar

- 2 cloves garlic, minced

- 1 tsp ginger, minced

- 2 tbsp olive oil

- Salt and pepper, to taste

Instructions:

1. In a bowl, combine Coconut Cream Pie Moonshine, coconut milk, soy sauce, brown sugar, garlic, and ginger.
2. Marinate chicken breasts in the mixture for at least 1 hour.
3. Heat olive oil in a skillet over medium heat. Add chicken breasts and cook until browned on both sides.
4. Pour in the marinade and simmer until chicken is cooked through and sauce has thickened.
5. Serve with rice and garnish with fresh cilantro or basil.

Ozark Distillery Coconut Moonshine Shrimp Stir-Fry

Ladies, gents, and lovers of maritime merriment, set sail for the culinary tropics with our Coconut Moonshine Shrimp Stir-Fry! This is not your average shrimp shuffle; it's a bold escapade in a pan, where the zest of the seven seas meets a whisper of island rebellion. Each succulent shrimp is sautéed to perfection, then flambeed in a splash of coconut moonshine, causing even the most stoic foodies to blush with delight.

Imagine the stir-fry as the stage, the shrimp kicking up their heels like a chorus line, and the vegetables twirling to the tune of tropical temptation—all wok-tossed in a sauce that's sweet, spicy, and spiked with enough moonshine to make the moon itself come down for a taste. It's a dish that promises to transport you to a beachside bonfire where the stars are bright, and the flavors are brighter. So, let's raise our forks and toast to a stir-fry that's not just good; it's coconutty, shrimptastic greatness in a bowl!

Ingredients:

- 1 lb large shrimp, peeled and deveined

- 1/3 cup Ozark Distillery Coconut Cream Pie Moonshine

- 2 tbsp sesame oil

- 1 bell pepper, sliced

- 1 zucchini, sliced

- 1 carrot, julienned

- 3 green onions, chopped

- 3 tbsp soy sauce

- 2 tbsp honey

Instructions:

1. In a bowl, mix Coconut Cream Pie Moonshine, soy sauce, and honey. Set aside.
2. Heat sesame oil in a large wok or skillet over high heat. Add shrimp and cook until pink.
3. Add bell pepper, zucchini, and carrot. Stir-fry for a few minutes.
4. Pour in the moonshine sauce mixture and stir well.
5. Cook until vegetables are tender and shrimp is coated with sauce.
6. Garnish with green onions and serve with steamed rice.

Ozark Distillery Coconut Moonshine Beef Curry

Prepare to have your culinary coconuts cracked by the one, the only, Coconut Moonshine Beef Curry! It's the dish that stared traditional curry in the face and said, "Let's get tropical." Picture your favorite tender, slow-cooked beef taking a detour through the Caribbean and picking up a hitchhiking bottle of moonshine along the way. It's a spice-laden, coconut cream-drenched extravaganza that'll have your taste buds swaying like a palm tree in a hurricane.

This curry doesn't tiptoe around your palate—it does the limbo under it, with just enough moonshine to make your inner pirate do a jig. Perfect for the adventurous eater who likes their meat with a side of mischief, this dish promises to be the life of the dinner party, telling saucy stories between mouthfuls. So, grab your spoon and a peg leg, and let's dig in— there's treasure in every bite!

Ingredients:

- 1 lb beef chunks

- 1/2 cup Ozark Distillery Coconut Cream Pie Moonshine

- 1 can coconut milk

- 2 tbsp curry powder

- 1 onion, chopped

- 2 cloves garlic, minced

- 1 tbsp ginger, minced

- 2 tbsp vegetable oil

- Salt and pepper, to taste

Instructions:

1. In a large pot, heat vegetable oil over medium heat. Add onion, garlic, and ginger. Sauté until translucent.
2. Add beef chunks and brown on all sides.
3. Add curry powder, stirring to coat the beef.
4. Pour in Coconut Cream Pie Moonshine and coconut milk. Bring to a boil.
5. Reduce heat and let simmer until beef is tender and sauce has thickened.
6. Season with salt and pepper. Serve with rice or naan.

Ozark Distillery Coconut Moonshine Salmon

Introducing the Coconut Moonshine Salmon – where the stream meets the dream, and your dinner plate becomes the stage for a culinary cabaret that's equal parts ocean and potion. This isn't your run-of-the-river fish dish; we've taken the lush, buttery richness of perfectly cooked salmon and given it a tropical twist that's as unexpected as finding a palm tree in a snowstorm. Marinated in a mischievous blend of coconut cream pie moonshine, this salmon brings a little bit of rebel to every flaky bite. Get ready to dive fork-first into an infusion of flavors that's sure to lure your taste buds into uncharted waters. It's more than a meal; it's a swim on the wild side, no lifejacket required. Bon appétit and anchors aweigh!

Ingredients:

- 4 salmon fillets
- 1/3 cup Ozark Distillery Coconut Cream Pie Moonshine
- 1/4 cup lime juice
- 2 tbsp honey
- 1 tsp chili flakes (optional for heat)
- Salt and pepper, to taste

Instructions:

1. In a bowl, mix together Coconut Cream Pie Moonshine, lime juice, honey, and chili flakes.
2. Season salmon fillets with salt and pepper.
3. Place salmon in a baking dish and pour the marinade over them.
4. Let marinate for 30 minutes.
5. Preheat the oven to 400°F (200°C).
6. Bake salmon for 12-15 minutes or until cooked through.
7. Serve with a side of steamed vegetables or salad.

Ozark Distillery Coconut Moonshine Rice Pudding

Saddle up for a spoonful of southern comfort twisted with tropical temptation in our Coconut Moonshine Rice Pudding. It's where down-home meets downtown, where the rice is soaked in a symphony of silky coconut milk and infused with a cheeky splash of moonshine, just enough to make your grandma blush and your taste buds do the Charleston. This isn't just a bowl of rice pudding; it's a culinary cuddle that packs a playful punch, a creamy concoction that whispers sweet nothings to your senses while winking at your wild side. Each spoonful is a warm hug followed by a high-five, the perfect comfort food for when you want to kick back, relax, and let the good times roll—one delightful bite at a time.

Ingredients:

- 1 cup Arborio rice

- 2 cups milk

- 1 cup coconut milk

- 1/2 cup Ozark Distillery Coconut Cream Pie Moonshine

- 1/3 cup sugar

- 1 tsp vanilla extract

- Toasted coconut flakes and cinnamon for garnish

Instructions:

1. In a saucepan, combine Arborio rice, milk, coconut milk, and sugar.
2. Bring to a low simmer, stirring often to prevent sticking.
3. Cook until the rice is tender and the mixture thickens (around 25-30 minutes).

4. Remove from heat and stir in the Coconut Cream Pie Moonshine and vanilla extract.
5. Transfer to serving dishes and chill for at least 2 hours.
6. Before serving, garnish with toasted coconut flakes and a sprinkle of cinnamon.

Ozark Distillery Coconut Moonshine Cheesecake

Say "aloha" to decadence with our Coconut Moonshine Cheesecake –
where tropical getaway meets backwoods hooch in a dessert so indulgent,
it ought to be against the law. This cheesecake is for those who take their
dessert like their adventures: wild, a little nutty, and with a kick that
sneaks up on you like a beachside sunset. Smooth, creamy, and spiked
with just the right amount of coconut moonshine, each slice is a wink at
the rules with a crust that crunches like sand under your toes. It's the
perfect rebel's reprieve for anyone looking to sweeten their day with a slice
of the illicit island life. Cheers to cheesecake that doesn't just sit on your
plate—it sways with the rhythm of a tropical breeze.

Ingredients:

- 1 1/2 cups graham cracker crumbs

- 1/2 cup melted butter

- 16 oz cream cheese, softened

- 1/2 cup sugar

- 2 eggs

- 1/4 cup Ozark Distillery Coconut Cream Pie Moonshine

- 1/4 cup coconut cream

- 1 tsp vanilla extract

- Toasted coconut flakes for topping

Instructions:

1. Preheat oven to 325°F (163°C).
2. Mix graham cracker crumbs and melted butter. Press into the bottom of a springform pan to form the crust.
3. In a large bowl, beat cream cheese and sugar until smooth.
4. Beat in eggs one at a time.
5. Add in Coconut Cream Pie Moonshine, coconut cream, and vanilla extract. Mix until smooth.
6. Pour the filling over the crust.
7. Bake for 45-50 minutes or until the center is set.
8. Let cool, then refrigerate for at least 4 hours or overnight.
9. Top with toasted coconut flakes before serving.

OZARK DISTILLERY COCONUT MOONSHINE MOLTEN LAVA CAKE

Prepare your dessert spoons for liftoff with the Coconut Moonshine Molten Lava Cake, a tropical eruption of flavor that's more thrilling than skinny dipping in a volcano. It's the cake that says, "Forget the beach; let's bake with a buzz!" Imagine the ooey-gooey center of a traditional molten lava cake, but with a coconutty, moonshine-kissed twist that flows like lava from a cakey crater – it's like a luau for your taste buds where the dress code strictly says "molten chic."

This cake doesn't just walk the line between dessert and cocktail, it conga-lines across it, offering a one-way ticket to a taste-tastic paradise. Every bite is a perfect balance of naughty and nice, the way grandma would've made it if she'd had a still in the backyard. So, tie on your apron, and let's get baking; because when coconut moonshine and chocolate collide, it's not just a cake – it's a celestial event in your mouth!

Ingredients:

- 1/2 cup butter

- 6 oz semi-sweet chocolate

- 2 eggs

- 2 egg yolks

- 1/4 cup sugar

- 2 tbsp Ozark Distillery Coconut Cream Pie Moonshine

- 3 tbsp all-purpose flour

- Pinch of salt

Instructions:

1. Preheat oven to 425°F (218°C).
2. Melt chocolate and butter together using a microwave or double boiler.
3. In a separate bowl, beat eggs, egg yolks, and sugar until pale and thick.
4. Gently fold in the melted chocolate mixture.
5. Add the Coconut Cream Pie Moonshine, flour, and salt. Mix until smooth.
6. Pour into greased ramekins.
7. Bake for 12-14 minutes, until the edges are firm but the center is soft.
8. Let sit for 1 minute, then invert onto plates. Serve immediately.

Ozark Distillery Bloody Mary Grilled Chicken

Introducing the Bloody Mary Grilled Chicken – a dish that's truly clucking fantastic! We've given boring grilled chicken the boot and invited it to a party at the grown-ups table. Each tender fillet is marinated in a concoction that's part tomato, and part secret spice mix that'll slap your taste buds awake faster than a Sunday morning hangover. This chicken comes off the grill with more lines than a Hollywood starlet and a flavor that's as bold as your Uncle Joe at family reunions. Perfect for those who like their poultry with a side of pizzazz, this bird is anything but the word. Get ready to raise your forks and toast to the chicken that's dressed to impress!

Ingredients:

- 4 boneless, skinless chicken breasts

- 1 cup Ozark Distillery Bloody Mary Mix

- 2 tbsp olive oil

- 1 tsp smoked paprika

- Salt and pepper, to taste

Instructions:

1. Marinate chicken breasts in Bloody Mary Mix for 3-4 hours.
2. Preheat grill to medium-high heat. Brush with olive oil to prevent sticking.
3. Season marinated chicken with smoked paprika, salt, and pepper.
4. Grill chicken for 6-8 minutes on each side or until fully cooked.
5. Serve with your preferred sides.

Ozark Distillery Bloody Mary Chili

Grab a spoon and say "Howdy!" to the wild child of comfort food: the Ozark Distillery Bloody Mary Chili! This ain't your mama's chili unless your mama wears cowboy boots to yoga and mixes her tomato juice with a side of mischief. This fiery concoction marries the heart-warming beans and beef of classic chili with the brunch-time boldness of a Bloody Mary. Each bite kicks like a mule and soothes like Sunday morning. It's like if your campfire decided to throw a brunch party and didn't invite the mild salsa. Served best with a wink, a smile, and perhaps a celery stick, this chili promises a culinary hoedown you won't soon forget. Oh Yeah

Ingredients:

- 1 lb ground beef

- 1 onion, diced

- 2 cloves garlic, minced

- 1 can (14 oz) diced tomatoes

- 1 can (14 oz) kidney beans, drained and rinsed

- 2 cups Ozark Distillery Bloody Mary Mix

- 1 tbsp chili powder

- 1 tsp cumin

- Salt and pepper, to taste

- Shredded cheese and sour cream for garnish

Instructions:

1. In a large pot, brown the ground beef over medium heat. Drain excess fat.
2. Add diced onion and minced garlic. Sauté until translucent.
3. Add diced tomatoes, kidney beans, Bloody Mary Mix, chili powder, and cumin. Stir well.
4. Bring the mixture to a boil, then reduce to a simmer and let cook for 30-40 minutes. Add water for preferred consistency.
5. Season with salt and pepper.
6. Serve with shredded cheese and sour cream on top.

Ozark Distillery Bloody Mary Meatloaf

Get ready to meatloaf like you've never meatloafed before with our Bloody Mary Meatloaf! This isn't your ordinary, diner-style brick of beef. Oh no, we've spiked the traditional family favorite with the peppery, celery-stalked swagger of a Sunday morning Bloody Mary. This loaf comes out of the oven juicier than a gossip columnist and spicier than a telenovela finale, ready to give your taste buds something to write home about.

Imagine: a crusty exterior that crunches like the ice in your glass, giving way to a moist, tender heart that's soaked up every herby, zesty note of your beloved brunch beverage. It's a meatloaf that doesn't just sit on your plate; it struts. So, slice into this boozy behemoth and let each bite transport you to a world where the meat is merry and every meal feels like a celebration. Cheers to that!

Ingredients:

- 1 lb ground beef

- 1/2 lb ground pork

- 1 cup breadcrumbs

- 1/2 cup Ozark Distillery Bloody Mary Mix

- 1 egg

- 1 onion, finely chopped

- 2 cloves garlic, minced

- 1 tbsp Worcestershire sauce

- Salt and pepper, to taste

Instructions:

1. Preheat oven to 375°F (190°C).
2. In a large bowl, combine all ingredients and mix well.
3. Form the mixture into a loaf and place in a baking dish.
4. Bake for 50-60 minutes or until the meatloaf is fully cooked.
5. Let rest for 10 minutes before slicing and serving.

OZARK DISTILLERY SPICY BLOODY MARY CHICKEN WINGS

Ladies and gentlemen, buckle up your taste buds and prepare for takeoff on Air Spicy Bloody Mary Chicken Wings, flying non-stop to Flavortown with a layover in Spiceville. These wings are not just a snack; they're a zesty, peppery, and oh-so-saucy adventure. Each wing is slathered in a Bloody Mary-inspired glaze that packs more punch than a heavyweight in a velvet robe, ensuring a takeoff so saucy, you'll need extra napkins for landing.

Our flight attendants will be by shortly with a round of napkins, because when it comes to our Spicy Bloody Mary Chicken Wings, it's less 'finger-licking good' and more 'face-planning fantastic.' So, strap in and get ready to deploy your tray tables, because these wings are about to bring a turbulence of flavor, you'll happily brave without a seatbelt. Welcome aboard the sauciest flight of your life—don't forget to enjoy the complimentary wet wipes!

Ingredients:

- 2 lbs chicken wings, separated at joints, tips removed

- 1 cup Ozark Distillery Spicy Bloody Mary Mix

- 2 tbsp olive oil

- Salt and pepper, to taste

- Celery sticks and blue cheese dressing for serving

Instructions:

1. Preheat oven to 425°F (220°C).
2. In a large bowl, toss chicken wings with Spicy Bloody Mary Mix, olive oil, salt, and pepper.

3. Spread wings on a baking sheet lined with parchment paper.
4. Bake for 25-30 minutes, turning once, until wings are cooked through and crispy.
5. Serve with celery sticks and blue cheese dressing.

OZARK DISTILLERY SPICY BLOODY MARY BEEF SKEWERS

Get ready to stick it to bland BBQs everywhere with our Spicy Bloody Mary Beef Skewers! Imagine your favorite steak-out getting crashed by the sassiest cocktail on the brunch block. These skewers have soaked up enough spicy tomato goodness to turn your grill into a confessional, where every "ooh" and "aah" forgives you for every overcooked burger of summers past. These beefy beauts are marinated in a zesty, peppery bath that's half Mary, half marauder, and they sizzle on the grill with the kind of sputter you usually hear after telling your aunt her Bloody Mary could use a little more "oomph." But beware, once off the grill, these spicy spears of carnivorous delight are liable to kick more than just flavor into your mouth – they've got enough kick to start a conga line on your tongue. So, skewer up, spice lovers, and get ready for a backyard feast that's part comedy, part culinary masterpiece, and entirely delicious.

Ingredients:

- 1 lb beef sirloin, cut into 1-inch cubes
- 1 cup Ozark Distillery Spicy Bloody Mary Mix
- 1 bell pepper, cut into 1-inch pieces
- 1 red onion, cut into 1-inch pieces
- Wooden skewers, soaked in water for 30 minutes

Instructions:

1. Marinate beef cubes in Spicy Bloody Mary Mix for 2-3 hours.
2. Preheat grill to medium-high heat.
3. Thread beef, bell pepper, and red onion alternately onto skewers.
4. Grill skewers for 10-12 minutes, turning occasionally, until beef reaches desired doneness.
5. Serve immediately.

Ozark Distillery Spicy Bloody Mary Shrimp Pasta

Dive fork-first into the audacious fusion of land and sea with the Ozark Distillery Spicy Bloody Mary Shrimp Pasta—a dish that's not just a meal, but a flavor expedition. This pasta tosses tradition overboard and invites your palate to a bold, briny feast where succulent shrimp tango with al dente noodles in a Spicy Bloody Mary embrace.

Ingredients:

- 8 oz linguine or spaghetti

- 1 lb large shrimp, peeled and deveined

- 1 cup Ozark Distillery Spicy Bloody Mary Mix

- 2 tbsp olive oil

- 3 cloves garlic, minced

- Fresh parsley, chopped for garnish

- Grated Parmesan cheese

Instructions:

1. Cook pasta according to package instructions. Drain.
2. In a skillet, heat olive oil over medium heat. Add garlic and sauté until fragrant.
3. Add shrimp and cook until they start to turn pink.
4. Pour in the Spicy Bloody Mary Mix and simmer until shrimp are cooked through.
5. Toss the sauce and shrimp with cooked pasta.
6. Serve garnished with fresh parsley and Parmesan cheese.

Ozark Distillery Spicy Bloody Mary Meatballs

Step right up for a bold twist on a cocktail classic with our Ozark Distillery Spicy Bloody Mary Meatballs! These aren't your grandma's Sunday supper meatballs; no sir, they've been given a jolt of life with the zingy, tangy, and oh-so-spicily divine flavors of a Bloody Mary. Handcrafted with the finest ground meat and seasoned to perfection, each meatball is infused with a hearty glug of Ozark Distillery's finest, bringing a peppery kick and a touch of firewater finesse to the mix.

Imagine these juicy orbs of deliciousness simmered in a sauce that's got all the trimmings of your beloved brunch cocktail—there's tomato, and there's spice that'll have your taste buds doing the two-step. Whether you're jazzing up a potluck or laying the smackdown on game day hunger, these Spicy Bloody Mary Meatballs are sure to be the MVP of the buffet table.

So, fire up the stove and get ready to roll out the most raucous meatballs this side of the Ozarks — where every bite is a little bit country, a little bit rock 'n roll, and a whole lotta delicious!

Ingredients:

- 1 lb ground beef

- 1/4 cup breadcrumbs

- 1 egg

- 1/4 cup grated Parmesan cheese

- 1 cup Ozark Distillery Spicy Bloody Mary Mix

- Salt and pepper, to taste

Instructions:

1. Preheat oven to 375°F (190°C).
2. In a bowl, combine ground beef, breadcrumbs, egg, Parmesan cheese, salt, and pepper. Mix until well combined.
3. Shape mixture into 1-inch meatballs and place on a baking sheet.
4. Bake for 20-25 minutes or until meatballs are browned and cooked through.
5. In a saucepan, heat Spicy Bloody Mary Mix over medium heat. Add baked meatballs and simmer for 10 minutes.
6. Serve hot.

Ozark Distillery Spicy Bloody Mary Vegetable Stir-Fry

Turn up the heat in your kitchen with our Spicy Bloody Mary Vegetable Stir-Fry, a vivacious veggie-packed dish that throws a party in the pan and invites all your taste buds to join the fun. This is not just a stir-fry; it's a fiesta of flavors, a veritable vegetable jubilee splashed with the bold zest of your favorite brunch cocktail!

Imagine crisp, colorful veggies tossed and sizzled to perfection, each piece coated in a sauce that's as lively and piquant as a Sunday morning Bloody Mary. The familiar kick of hot sauce, the tang of tomato, and a whisper of Worcestershire dance together in a medley that brings the sassy, savory notes of the iconic drink straight to your plate.

Perfect for the adventurous foodie looking to shake up their meal prep routine, this Spicy Bloody Mary Vegetable Stir-Fry is a culinary conga line of fresh ingredients and bold spices that'll have your fork doing the tango. So, grab your skillet, and let's set the stove to "sizzle" — it's time to stir-fry with a splash of spirit!

Ingredients:

- 2 cups mixed vegetables (bell peppers, broccoli, snap peas, etc.)

- 3/4 cup Ozark Distillery Spicy Bloody Mary Mix

- 2 tbsp soy sauce

- 1 tbsp olive oil

- 2 cloves garlic, minced

- Cooked rice for serving

Instructions:

1. In a large skillet or wok, heat olive oil over medium-high heat. Add garlic and sauté until fragrant.
2. Add mixed vegetables and stir-fry for 5-7 minutes or until they start to soften.
3. Pour in the Spicy Bloody Mary Mix and soy sauce. Stir well and continue to cook until vegetables are tender and the sauce has thickened.
4. Serve over cooked rice.

As we reach the final pages of "The Spirit of Ozark Distillery: A Culinary Adventure," we hope the journey has been as enriching for you as the flavors are complex in the recipes we've shared. From the robust, warm notes of our small-batch bourbon to the smooth whisper of our meticulously crafted vodka, each Ozark Distillery spirit has been a steadfast companion in our culinary quests.

Throughout this adventure, hopefully you have learned to mix and mingle ingredients but also to appreciate the intricate dance of flavors that bring life to both plate and glass. We've celebrated the heritage of the Ozark region, its abundant natural beauty, and the unwavering spirit of its people—a spirit distilled into every bottle that comes from your friends at Ozark Distillery.

Each recipe is a story told through the senses, a testament to the versatility and depth that our hand-crafted spirits can bring to the table. We've witnessed the transformation of simple meals into memorable feasts, and classic cocktails into innovative concoctions that echo the whispers of tradition while singing with a modern flair.

But, as with any good spirit, the essence lies not just in its solitary enjoyment but in the shared experience it brings. These recipes are more than a collection of instructions; they are an invitation to gather, to laugh, to share, and to create memories. The Spirit of Ozark Distillery is as much about community as it is about culinary exploits—each sip and every bite is a call for togetherness.

As you close this book, remember that the adventure doesn't end here. The true spirit of Ozark Distillery extends beyond these pages, flourishing wherever there are curious souls ready to explore the art of good eating and the craft of Ozark Distillery.

May you carry the spirit of this book into your kitchen and beyond, allowing the rich tastes and aromatic pleasures to infuse your life with the warmth and joy that is the essence of the Ozarks. Until our next adventure, may your glasses remain raised, your plates forever plentiful, and your hearts open to the endless adventures that await.

David W Huffman Sr & Tiffhany Huffman

Printed in the USA
CPSIA information can be obtained
at www.ICGtesting.com
LVHW020731260424
778410LV00011B/315